THE POCKET
UNIVERSAL
METHODS
OF DESIGN

125 Ways to Research Complex Problems, Develop
Innovative Ideas, and Design Effective Solutions

Bruce Hanington   Bella Martin

ROCKPORT

Contents

A/B Testing

Comparing two versions of a design to see which performs better against a predetermined goal

- A/B testing is an optimization technique that allows you to compare two different versions of a design to see which one gets you closer to a business objective.

- Tests are run by randomly assigning different people down two paths—the "A" test and the "B" test—until a statistically relevant sample size is reached.

- Testing can assess design aspects such as different treatments of text copy (tone, length, and font size); form elements (how many, layout, and which are required); and different treatments of the button or call to action (page placement, size, color, and labeling).

- A/B testing won't help you understand why the design was preferred over the alternate, so pair it with qualitative methods to gain a deeper understanding of customer trust, desires, attitudes, and needs.

See also   Experiments • Key Performance Indicators • Web Analytics

An eBay study comparing image size determined that users
were more engaged with larger images, even though it
sacrificed the amount of information contained to one page,
contradicting research expectations.

AEIOU

A framework for structuring field observations

- AEIOU can be used to guide any ethnographic or observational method, corresponding to five interrelated elements:

  - **Activities** are goal-directed sets of actions or the pathways that people take toward the things they want to accomplish.

  - **Environments** include the context in which activities take place, including the atmosphere and function of individual and shared spaces.

  - **Interactions** are the routine and special exchanges between people and between people and objects in the environment.

  - **Objects** are the key elements of the environment, sometimes put to complex or even unintended uses.

  - **Users** are the people whose behaviors, preferences, and needs are being observed, including their roles and relationships.

See also   Contextual Inquiry • Fly-on-the-Wall Observation • Observation

Fieldwork observations of Activities, Environments, Interactions, Objects, and Users are converged onto a team worksheet for synthesis and analysis by the design team.

Affinity Diagramming

The visible clustering of observations and insights into meaningful categories and relationships

- Designers capture research insights, observations, concerns, or requirements on individual sticky notes.

- Rather than grouping notes into predefined categories, specific details are clustered, which then give rise to named category themes based on shared affinity of similar intent, issues, or problems.

- Making tacit knowledge or information buried in transcripts visible facilitates research synthesis.

- Affinity diagramming from contextual inquiry is based on interviews and observations of users in the field, synthesizing human stories.

- Affinity diagramming from usability testing documents observations and quotes of participant task performance to determine priority issues to be fixed.

- Color-coded sticky notes can help to efficiently parse information by user, task, or issue.

See also   Content Analysis • Contextual Design • KJ Technique

Observations from multiple usability tests at Citrix are color-coded by participant, prioritizing issues to be revised and retested.

Artifact Analysis

A systematic examination of the material, aesthetic, and interactive qualities of objects

- Artifact analysis asks what objects say about people and their culture, time, and place rather than focusing on what people say about the products and systems they use.

- Material analysis addresses the quantity, material composition, physical and digital components, durability, wear patterns, and disposability of objects.

- Aesthetic analysis includes subjective assessment of form, color, texture, references to particular eras, time, or place, and emotional significance.

- Interactive aspects of the analysis address the characteristics of operational use and behaviors that the artifact affords: for example, function and complexity.

- Contextual aspects include where objects are stored or carried, if they are part of a larger whole, and if they are owned, shared, public, or private property.

- Identifying object misuse or adapted use can suggest design opportunities.

See also Personal Inventories • Touchstone Tours • Unobtrusive Measures

Artifact analysis is a systematic examination of the material, aesthetic, and interactive qualities of objects in context.

Automated Remote Research

Using web-based tools to reveal statistically relevant data for usability enhancements

- Automated remote research enables design teams to leverage web-based tools to collect statistically significant information about what people are doing on your website or web application.

- Focus is on planning the appropriate strategy for the study, accurately selecting the right automated remote research tools, and configuring the logistics.

- Automated research tools can help researchers understand usability issues such as length of time and performance on task, common click paths, and trouble spots.

- It should be used with qualitative research methods that provide insight into why site visitors behave the way they do.

- Quantitative data can be triangulated with observed behavioral data to decide which enhancements to make.

- There are a growing number of web-based research tools available that are both quantitative and qualitative.

See also   Crowdsourcing • Experiments • Remote Moderated Research

QUALITATIVE (MODERATED)

Remote Screen-Sharing:
Adobe Connect, GoToMeeting, NetMeeting, LiveLook,
Uservue, Skype, WebEx, Glance, Yuuguu, etc.

OpenHallway

CONCRETE

Live Sites / Apps Wireframes

Conceptual artifacts Surveys

CONCEPTUAL

UserZoom
RelevantView
WebEffective
Webnographer

Chalkmark
Usabilia

Online Card Sorting:
Optimal Sort
WebSort

SurveyMonkey
SurveyGizmo
PollDaddy, etc.

ClickTale
ClickHeat, etc.

A/B/C Testing

Web
Analytics

QUANTITATIVE (AUTOMATED)

Web Surveys

This is a framework of different types of remote research tools
and applications. Automated remote methods are shown
toward the bottom half of the diagram.

Backcasting

The process of looking backward in time from an assumed set of circumstances in a future time, to better understand what could lead there, in order to explore appropriate intervention

- Backcasting relates to Scenarios: the creation and maintenance of a plurality of forward views and alternative theories of how change might unfold.

- Backcasting also relates to Visioning: the elaboration of a preferred scenario that can be used to make plans.

- Backcasting includes development of participatory approaches incorporating perspectives from diverse stakeholders.

- The management and foresight method "Three Horizons" divides the change process into three phases: now (horizon one), then (horizon three), and the interim phase between (horizon two). It provides a way of attending to and creating a narrative out of whatever is really at stake in transitioning from one state of affairs to another.

Contributed by Stuart Candy

See also   Horizon Scanning • Scenarios • Transition Design

Present · TRANSITION PATHWAY · Desired Futures

Courtesy of Terry Irwin

Different types of projects are linked to each other via mid- and long-term co-created visions. These "ecologies" of projects and initiatives become "steps" along the transition pathway toward the desired midterm future.

Behavioral Design

The intentional use of design to influence people's behavior, translating insights from different disciplines into design techniques applicable to interfaces, products, services, and environments

- Behavioral design involves a multidisciplinary approach, drawing on knowledge and models from other fields relating to how people think and act, and applying those insights in design.

- There are some useful cross-domain, cross-disciplinary concepts to frame our thinking about how to influence behavior through design, such as *enabling* (making a certain behavior easier for someone to do), *motivating* (trying to get someone to want to perform or not perform a particular behavior), and *constraining* (making an undesired behavior harder to do).

- The *Design with Intent* toolkit illustrated here provides a "pattern library" for brainstorming, exploring problem-solution spaces, and classifying existing ideas, drawing on examples and insights from different disciplines.

Contributed by Dan Lockton

See also   Behavioral Mapping • Design Ethnography • Unobtrusive Measures

The *Design with Intent* toolkit groups 101 design patterns, through eight lenses, for influencing behavior, drawn from a variety of disciplinary perspectives.

Behavioral Mapping

Systematic visual documentation of location-based human activity

- Behavioral mapping is used to document observable human activities and personal characteristics, interactions, time spent at fixed locations or in transit, and details of environmental context.

- A sketch map or architectural floor plan is used as the underlay for recording observations.

- Place-centered mapping is based on observations of all people and their interactions at a specific location.

- Individual-centered mapping follows the travel and activities of specific individuals over time and location, documenting their social behaviors and interactions.

- While typically completed in real time, mapping can involve time-lapse photography or video.

- Interviews or debriefing conversations with participants help to understand more about mapped behaviors.

- In retrospective mapping, individuals chart their own paths and behaviors on a floor plan or map, revealing their motivations for actions.

See also Fly-on-the-Wall Observation • Shadowing • Unobtrusive Measures

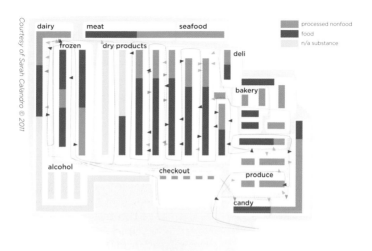

dairy | meat | seafood

frozen | dry products | deli

bakery

alcohol | checkout | produce

candy

processed nonfood
food
n/a substance

▶ Participant 1
31 items total =
17 food +
14 sad nonfood

▶ Participant 2
13 items total =
7 food +
6 sad nonfood

▶ Participant 3
40 items total =
16 food +
34 sad nonfood

Behavioral mapping of consumer routes in a grocery store are combined with shadowing observations and conversation to establish a picture of shopping patterns.

Blockbusting

Tactics to remove hindrances to problem solving and broaden creative thinking

- Perceptual blocks can hinder clear perception of problem spaces. Adams defines six types of blocks:

  - **Narrow Stereotyping** Defaulting to expectations can lead to stereotyping and labeling.

  - **Ineffective Scoping** Too broad or narrow a scale may cause ideas to be ruled out early, or misplace the focus.

  - **Limiting Frame** Problem-solvers prototype concepts by leveraging features they deem essential, then exclude the components identified as essential.

  - **Singular Viewing** Problem-solvers frequently struggle to see tasks from various viewpoints. Role-play relevant activities as various stakeholders.

  - **Minimal Recalling of Content** Determine this block by recording a task relying on memory alone and assess what is missed.

  - **Poorly Engaging Senses** Consider generating a range of concepts, each leveraging a different sense.

Contributed by Stacie Rohrbach

See also   Brainstorm Graphic Organizers •
Design Workshops • Parallel Prototyping

MAKE LIP
SPILL-
PROOF

WIDEN
HANDLE
OPENING

BROADEN
BASE

EASY TO
CARRY

INSULATED FOR
WARM/COOL
LIQUIDS

BACKPACK
WATER
CARRIER

STRAW SPOUT
TO COMBAT
SPILLING

INEFFECTIVE SCOPING

HOLES FOR
BREAD

HEATING
ELEMENT

LEVER

ELECTRIC
PLUG

HOLD
BREAD
IN PLACE

TOASTER
TONGS!

LIMITING FRAME

Some examples of workshop activities for blockbusting.

Bodystorming

Brainstorming and spontaneous prototyping through dynamic physical experience and role-play

- Designers immerse themselves in user situations through simulated contexts while paying close attention to decisions, interactive experiences, and emotional responses.

- Concept ideas can be integrated and tested in play, and the active situation can inspire the spontaneous creation of new product and service concepts.

- Bodystorming prototypes use simple constructions and props at hand: for example, cardboard, boxes, existing objects, furniture, and lighting manipulations.

- While scenarios may be partially scripted from observations, the bodystorm encourages improvisation to capture real-world experiences.

- The method may be contained within design teams but can also engage a wider audience of peers or clients, inviting response and dialogue.

See also   Experience Prototyping • Role-playing • Simulations

Designers bodystorm an alarm system with personal bubbles of sound space controlled by mobile devices, awakening one person while a roommate continues to sleep.

Brainstorm Graphic Organizers

Visual structures of new ideas and concepts

- Brainstorming creates a judgment-free zone to express creative ideas and explore new concepts.

- Widely accepted rules include, "quantity over quality," "withhold judgment and criticism," "build on each other's ideas," and "welcome oddity."

- Graphic organizers, or visual representations of knowledge, are sense-making frameworks that facilitate teams as they brainstorm unconventional alternatives within a domain.

- **Brainstorming Webs** help develop a central concept or question, identifying its characteristics, supporting facts, and related ideas.

- **Tree Diagrams** communicate hierarchy, a classification system, or relationships between main and supporting ideas.

- **Flow Diagrams** document a sequence of events, represent the actions or processes of different actors in a system, or show cause and effect of interrelated elements.

See also Cognitive Mapping • Concept Mapping • Mind Mapping

Webs, Trees, and Flow Diagrams provide sense-making frameworks for facilitating and visualizing brainstorming, disrupting and challenging old patterns of thinking.

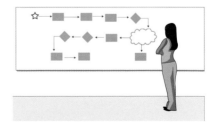

Brand Experience Workshop

Discussions about well-known brands and products to help create a shared vision about a new product experience before the design process begins

- The brand experience workshop is based on a broad selection of brand and product representations. Each brand image, word, or description conveys an emotion or quality of interaction.

- Before the workshop, print out a set of about 100 emotion-inducing images representing well-known products and services.

- Give each participant 10–25 red and green dot stickers. Instruct them to follow their gut reactions and place the stickers directly onto the images (red for undesirable, green for desirable).

- The facilitator guides a discussion by creating a continuum along the wall.

- Record the adjectives and words people are using.

- After the workshop, synthesize the results and come up with a set of adjectives that capture the brand.

Contributed by Barbora Batokova

See also   Design Workshops • Picture Cards • Value Opportunity Analysis

Participants use red and green dot stickers to rate images based on how they feel about a brand. Encourage participants to use their gut and not overthink their decisions too much, because the images will be used to guide the discussion after.

The resulting brand image continuum maps the images from undesirable to desirable based on the perceived attributes from participants.

Bull's-Eye Diagramming

A method to prioritize a data set using a target diagram

- To create effective solutions, designers must understand what's important and deprioritize the rest.

- Bull's-Eye Diagramming helps us achieve clarity and focus by arranging items (e.g., product features, user needs, pain points, etc.) in order of importance.

- The two most common ways to use the diagram are as a **team activity** to develop a plan of action or achieve shared understanding through a productive discussion, and as a **design discovery tool with participants** to uncover people's priorities or beliefs about a topic.

- Achieving consensus can be challenging; however, being part of the prioritization process allows everyone to be heard and feel included.

- With the discovery activity, in silence, a participant uses the diagram to assign rank to items based on their personal preference, values, relevance, importance, etc.

Contributed by Barbora Batokova

See also   Importance-Difficulty Matrix • Kano Analysis • Values-based Assessment

(left) You can use predefined templates for this method or draw a set of concentric circles on a white board or butcher paper for the activity.

(right) The "What's on Your Radar?" template provides space for specifying the task or question for participants when you're using this method as a design discovery tool.

Business Origami

Paper-prototyping interactions and value exchanges among people, artifacts, and environments

- Business origami is a service design activity where stakeholders build a physical representation of a system and then prototype future or alternative states.

- Paper tokens represent actors, artifacts, environments, and technologies on a horizontal whiteboard "stage" where interactions play out to tell a story.

- Lines and arrows labeled on the whiteboard represent the interactions between tokens, articulating what value people get out of the exchange.

- The method gives all participants an equal voice in the prototyping activity, bridging different perspectives by providing a common reference for further discussion.

- The experience of physical modeling is critical, making the value exchange explicit within a scenario.

See also   Creative Toolkits • Design Workshops • User Journey Maps

Paper pop-up "origami" tokens represent people, locations, artifacts, technology, transportation, channels, third parties, social media, and proprietary tools, with lines and arrows illustrating relationships.

Card Sorting

Participant sorting of concepts, terms, or features into meaningful categories and relationships using printed cards

- Card sorting is used to explore how participants group items into categories and relate concepts to one another, whether for digital interface design or a table of contents.

- It can be used to identify terminology that is vague, misunderstood, or has multiple meanings associated with it.

- Card sorting can also be used to generate options for structuring information, identifying different schemas for organizing navigation, menus, and taxonomies.

- It validates that the categories in your product or service reflect the mental model of your audience.

- Including blank cards and markers allows participants to add their own items where needed.

- If no consistent patterns emerge after several card sorts, consider renaming the cards or reconsider the categories.

See also   Automated Remote Research •
Content Inventory & Audit • Desirability Testing

Card sorting can help you understand how people group information, perceive and describe different groups of information, and generate ideas for navigation categories.

Case Studies

In-depth investigation of single instances to gain detailed knowledge using multiple sources

- Case studies are useful for understanding existing phenomena for comparison or inspiration and to study the effects of change, new programs, or innovations.

- Instances, or cases, may be of individuals, events, organizations, entire communities, or processes.

- Details of cases emerge during data collection and analysis, which typically include the following features:

  - Selection of a case or small set of cases

  - Study of the case in its social and physical context

  - Collection of information using multiple, triangulated methods such as interviews, observations, unobtrusive trace measures, and document analysis

- This method welcomes extraordinary cases and outliers rather than looking for representative instances.

- Similar to the design process, case studies require the researcher to determine a problem, make hypotheses, conduct research, revise theory, and tell a story.

See also   Evidence-based Design • Research Through Design • Secondary Research

When well composed and designed, case studies can result in compelling human narratives, with vivid details that make the case more memorable.

Civic Design & Policy

The promotion of new forms of grassroots citizen engagement in community and nonprofits, and design practice within public or government institutions

- **Design for civic engagement** is the endeavor taken by designers promoting participation and new forms of citizen engagement at the grassroots level.

- **Design for policy or government** is the practice developed within public or government-affiliated institutions. Designers in this realm have found space to work within innovation teams, service creation and delivery, and policy implementation teams.

- Design within the civic and political realm is changing the way citizens organize at the local level and is shifting the way public services are delivered and public servants are ideating on the creation and implementation of policies.

Contributed by Sofía Bosch Gómez and Marysol Ortega Pallanez

See also   Participatory Design • Service Blueprint • Service Design

Courtesy of Francis Carter

Artists, health and wellness representatives, non-profits, and members of the Bronx community plan Play Streets day, which creates safe community play environments by closing down normally car-filled streets.

Children drawing during the Play Streets event.

Drawings made by children in the community were used to explore possible and plausible implementation with adult stakeholders.

Cognitive Mapping

A visualization technique that reveals how people process and make sense of their experience

- Cognitive maps are most effective when used to structure complex problems.

- It is designed specifically as a decision-making tool that can inform strategic direction.

- Unlike concept maps or mind maps, the format and structure require no central focus of visualization.

- Nodes of a cognitive map are made up of the exact words and phrases spoken by participants.

- Each node can have as many incoming and outgoing associations as necessary and are read as causal pathways: for example, *node x may imply node y*.

- Cognitive mapping can facilitate the note-taking process during interviews and when transcribing text-based qualitative data.

See also   Concept Mapping • Content Analysis • Mind Mapping

Cognitive Map courtesy of Luiz Flávio Autran Monteiro Gomes, Luís Alberto Duncan Rangel, and Rogério Lúcio Jerônimo

Cognitive maps reveal people's underlying agendas and decision-making criteria. This map is based on a questionnaire for employees considering leaving a company headquarters.

Cognitive Walkthrough

Evaluating whether the order of prompts in a system reflects the way people cognitively process tasks

- A cognitive walkthrough is a usability inspection method that evaluates a system's anticipated ease-of-use without instruction, coaching, or training.

- Each step of the interaction with the system can be assessed as a step that either moves the individual closer to or further from their goal.

- Evaluators ask four questions for each step in the sequence:

  1. Will users want to produce whatever effect the action has?

  2. Will users see the control (button, menu, label, etc.) for the action?

  3. Will users recognize that the control will produce the effect that they want?

  4. Will users understand feedback they get, so they can confidently continue on to the next action?

- It should be used with usability testing to uncover different classes of design issues and problems.

See also   Heuristic Evaluation • Think-aloud Protocol • Wizard of Oz

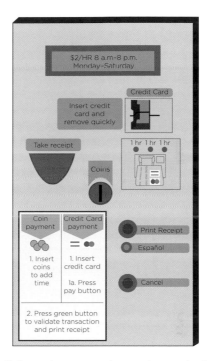

Cognitive walkthroughs are used to evaluate whether an interface is understandable and easy to learn based on the user's problem-solving mental operations.

Collage

The visual expression of thoughts, feelings, desires, and other aspects of life using images and words

- A collage can help mitigate the limitations of traditional verbal means in gathering innermost thoughts.

- The paper canvas may be blank, or it may have lines to suggest placement such as past, present, and ideal future.

- Collage kits should have images and words ambiguous enough to avoid bias, yet specific enough to be relevant.

- Blank frames or stickers and markers should be included for participants to add their own material.

- A single person usually completes a collage, but sessions are generally conducted in small groups.

- Participants present their collages to the group, providing insight about choices for analysis.

- Qualitative analysis is used to look for patterns and themes within and across several collages, such as use or non-use of elements, placement, and relationship.

See also   Creative Toolkits • Generative Research •
Participatory Design

Collage allows participants to project their thoughts, feelings, and desires onto a visual artifact, providing insight and inspiration for design teams.

Competitive Testing

Research to evaluate the usability and learnability of your competitors' products

- Competitive testing complements traditional marketing strategies and business audits by considering the social, economic, and technical context.

- It allows design teams to assess a competitor's products from the end user's point of view.

- Teams inspect how usable and learnable competitors' digital applications are by conducting usability tests on competitive products, as well as on their own.

- In contrast to attitudinal surveys, competitive testing focuses on end-user behavior as people attempt to accomplish tasks that exist across products.

- By understanding key similarities and differences between competitors, gaps can be identified for further market differentiation or specialization.

- Results from competitive tests should be ongoing, tracked, and compared over time.

See also   Kano Analysis • Think-aloud Protocol • Value Opportunity Analysis

Before designing a shopping assistant for a retail warehouse environment, a design team conducted competitive research of existing, in-store help kiosks.

Concept Mapping

A visual framework connecting a large number of ideas, objects, and events as they relate to a certain domain

- Concept mapping provides scaffolding that can help visualize the complexities of a system to make new meaning.

- Concept maps consist of individual concepts (a well-understood idea, object, or event; usually nouns connected by linking words (usually verbs).

- Linking words that connect two or more concepts form a proposition that creates a meaningful statement.

- Articulating the correct focus question is a key step that will provide context and structure to the map.

- After a focus question is generated, a list of fifteen to twenty-five concepts should be identified and ranked from general to very specific.

- A preliminary map is constructed and then revised until a final map emerges to \ answer the focus questions.

- Maps should help design teams gain new knowledge and find new meanings in an information space.

See also Brainstorm Graphic Organizers • Cognitive Mapping • Mind Mapping

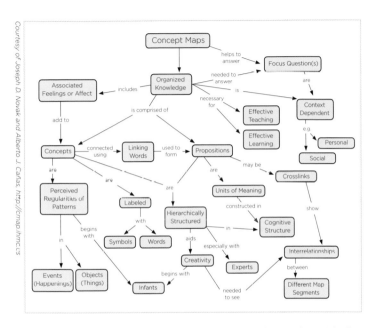

Concept maps are organized in a downward hierarchy, with the focus question at the top of the map and the most general concepts below it.

Content Analysis

The systematic description of form and content of written, spoken, or visual materials expressed in themes, patterns, and counts

- Content analysis provides an established and systematic technique for dealing with qualitative data.

- In inductive content analysis, the categories or codes are derived from a systematic reading of a sample set of the materials to be analyzed.

- In deductive content analysis, codes or categories are derived beforehand, often based on a theoretical framework.

- Content analysis can identify themes and patterns in the data, including how dominantly they are represented.

- Outcomes can be quantitative, counting occurrences of the words, phrases, images, or concepts.

- The method also examines form and structure of communication: for example, scale and location of images or the font and type size of text.

- For smaller sample sets, content analysis can be done manually; for larger sets, software is available.

See also   Affinity Diagramming • Thematic Networks • Word Clouds

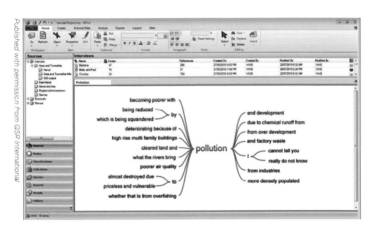

Content analysis helps you extract themes and make meaning out of unstructured information, often with the help of software. *Shown: Word tree from NVivo 9.*

Content Inventory & Audit

A content inventory tells you what your content is; an audit recommends what it should be

- Everything a customer can read, watch, interact with, or listen to can be considered content.

- Perform an inventory and audit:

  - When beginning a website redesign

  - When merging multiple sites or splitting up into smaller, niche sites

  - When preparing content for multichannel distribution or a Content Management System (CMS)

- A content inventory organizes assets into a spreadsheet of content items and attributes.

- A quantitative content audit assesses the attributes of "Governance," including ownership, copyright, and creative details.

- The qualitative content audit rates "Content Quality" criteria such as credibility, originality, accuracy, and relevance to identify unifying themes and patterns across content sources.

See also Card Sorting • Key Performance Indicators • Site Search Analytics

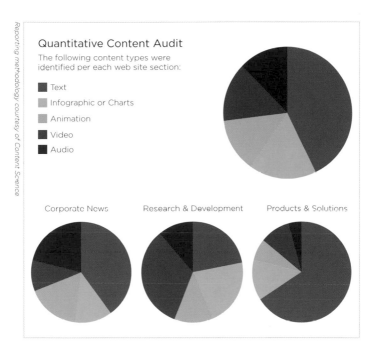

Reporting methodology courtesy of Content Science

Quantitative Content Audit

The following content types were identified per each web site section:

- ■ Text
- ■ Infographic or Charts
- ■ Animation
- ■ Video
- ■ Audio

Corporate News   Research & Development   Products & Solutions

Content inventories and audits can provide quantitative and qualitative visualizations to help stakeholders understand where content stands and where it needs to be.

Contextual Design

A customer-centered process that makes designer workflow concrete, explicit, and sharable

- Designers intuitively understand the leap from customer-centered data to a sound design direction, but to non-designers this process can seem "fuzzy" or "magic."

- Recommended steps to make design work more predictable and inclusive of non-designers include:

  - *Contextual Inquiry* to understand the customer

  - *Interpretation Sessions* for each customer interview

  - *Work Models and Affinity Diagrams* to represent the complex systems of work

  - *Visioning and Storyboarding* to generate concepts to support the customer's work

  - *User Environment Design* to document natural flow of the customer's work

  - *Paper Mock-ups* to get feedback from customers before coding and implementation

- The process can reduce the time it takes to move through customer-centered design challenges.

See also Affinity Diagramming • Contextual Inquiry • Storyboards

Contextual Design process steps

Requirements & Solutions

Contextual Inquiry	Talk to specific customers in the field	1
Interpretation Session	Interpret the data as a team to capture issues	
Work Models & Affinity Diagramming	Consolidate data across customers for a full market view	
Visioning	Redesign people's work with new technology ideas	2

Define & Validate Concepts

Storyboarding	Work out the details of particular tasks and roles	
User Environment Design	Design system to support this work	3
Paper Mock-Up Interviews	Mock up the interface using interaction patterns for testing	
Interaction & Visual Design	Design and test the final look and user experience	4

Contextual design is a customer-centered process that begins with data from contextual inquiry, intended to help with transitions between common steps of the design process.

Contextual Inquiry

An immersive, contextual way to observe and interview that reveals underlying work structure

- Four principles define the contextual inquiry method:

  1. **Context:** To understand the ongoing experience and tacit knowledge of the worker, it is critical that the researcher observe details in context.

  2. **Partnership:** This is similar to a master/apprentice model, watching, asking questions, and seeking to understand how the data more reliably reflects reality.

  3. **Interpretation:** What researchers see and hear must be interpreted for meaning and double-checked with participants on-site.

  4. **Focus:** The researcher must learn to expand beyond personal focus to see more in the participant's world, picking up on idiosyncrasies and contradictions.

- This is used to understand communication flows, sequence of tasks, artifacts, tools, and the influence of culture and the physical environment on work.

- Interview multiple people in different user segments before synthesizing contextual inquiry findings.

See also Affinity Diagramming • Contextual Design • Interviews

Contextual Inquiry provides a way to structure interviews with people that reveal specific details about how they work and helps expose underlying work structure.

027

Creative Matrix

A visual structure that helps generate a wide range of ideas at the intersections of various categories

- To create solutions that we never imagined might be possible, we must break away from conventional thinking.

- To start, draw a large grid of rows and columns and label it: columns are categories related to people (e.g., challenges, pain points, market segments, or personas) and rows are categories enabling solutions (e.g., spaces, technologies, activities, or policies).

- Next, organize participants into teams of 4 to 6 people and instruct everyone to generate as many ideas as they can in silence for 15 to 20 minutes.

- An effective way to populate the matrix with novel ideas is to transform the project's problem statements into How Might We (HMW) statements.

- Include categories that are seemingly unrelated and designate one row as a wild card for ideas.

Contributed by Barbora Batokova

See also   How Might We • KJ Technique • Weighted Matrix

In a relatively short time, many ideas can be generated at the intersections of problem statements with categories that enable solutions.

028

Creative Toolkits

Collections of physical elements organized for participatory modeling, visualization, or creative play

- Facilitated participatory exercises can provide people with a tangible artifact on which to project thoughts, feelings, desires, and emotions.

- Flexible or Velcro modeling kits contain a range of three-dimensional forms, buttons, and ambiguous design elements that can be easily configured.

- Interface kits can contain paper or card elements representing design features for flexible arrangement, suggesting mock or ideal web or device interactions.

- Collage kits can contain an inventory of images and words or shape and symbol elements for open interpretation and use relevant to the design inquiry.

- Drawing kits will contain various papers, cards, and writing tools accommodating a range of potential exercises.

- Depending on the intent of the exercise, kits can be built from original materials or from existing parts, toys, or games.

See also Design Workshops • Generative Research • Participatory Design

Here is a typical Velcro modeling kit with form and element variations designed for physical manipulation and configuration by participants.

029

Critical Incident Technique

Understanding how users experience your product at critical moments to optimize future designs

- Ask individuals to describe a situation with your product or service.

- Collect positive and negative experiences through directed storytelling, interviews, or diary studies to identify:

  - *The incident cause:* What were the events leading up to the critical incident?

  - *User actions:* What were the behaviors that took place during the incident?

  - *User sentiment:* How did the user feel during the incident and afterward?

  - *Incident outcome:* Did the user change how he or she behaved after the incident?

  - *Ideal outcome:* What are possible future outcomes?

- Representative scenarios cover possible explanations and recommendations.

- Prioritize and triangulate with other research to gain a better understanding of situations that have a profound impact on user behavior.

See also   Diary Studies • Directed Storytelling • Interviews

The Critical Incident Technique focuses on how people solve problems, with the goal of optimizing and re-creating successful results and eliminating the negative, counterproductive ones.

030

Critiques

A central mechanism to advance the design process, inviting constructive feedback on concepts from teachers, clients, stakeholders, or peers

- The open critique of shared work is a unique feature of design and related creative fields.

- Lerman outlines a series of steps with specified roles of the artist or designer, responders, and a facilitator:

  1. **Statements of Meaning:** Responders indicate what they found meaningful, interesting, or remarkable about the work.

  2. **Designer Questions:** The designer asks questions of the responders. Responders may provide opinions only in direct response to questions.

  3. **Neutral Questions:** Responders ask neutral questions of the designer; for example, rather than "Why did you choose red?" they would ask, "What informed your choice of colors?"

  4. **Permissioned Opinions:** Responders state, "I have an opinion about _____. Would you like to hear it?" The designer has the option of saying yes or no.

See also Design Charette • Design Workshops • Stakeholder Walkthrough

Various forms of critique include the desk critique or expert review, public or peer critique, and client reviews.

031

Crowdsourcing

Voluntary completion of tasks or micro-projects by an undefined, large group of people

- Crowdsourcing brings together users and testers to evaluate prototypes and submit potential solutions to problems.

- Micro-tasks are accessed via a common platform that can be completed by volunteers within seconds or minutes.

- Participants receive monetary (a micropayment) or nonmonetary (reputation points) compensation.

- Design straightforward, uncomplicated tasks to get the most volunteers to participate.

- Include questions that have a bona-fide answer as part of the task to prevent volunteers from "gaming" the system by entering nonsense responses.

- Devise tasks so that completing them correctly and in good faith requires as much or even less work than entering random, invalid responses.

- Consider triangulation with other methods to increase confidence of research outcomes.

See also Automated Remote Research • Photo Studies • Triangulation

Using crowdsourcing, frog's frogMob invites people from all over the world to upload their photographs of interesting trends to inform and inspire designers.

032

Cultural Probes

Provocative instruments to inspire new forms of self-understanding and communication

- Use materials such as postcards, journals, cameras, text, and imagery to gather personal insights from participants.

- Provocations are designed to inspire people to thoughtfully consider personal context and circumstance and respond in unique, creative ways.

- Materials should be varied and imaginative to elicit responses that are relevant to the design inquiry.

- Probes are flexible, open-ended, and intentionally subjective, collecting inspirational data to stimulate design imagination.

- Design probes support empathic understanding through information gathering over a prolonged period, where the researcher cannot be present.

- Probe kits are combined with other research methods such as observations, site visits, and interviews.

- Probes should be thoughtful in aesthetic craft, message, and delivery and be created to inspire delight and respect, response, and return.

See also Diary Studies • Experience Sampling Method • Photo Studies

A study on mass customization of products collected personal stories of participants using a cultural probe kit of digital voice recorders, cameras, postcards, diaries, and stickers.

033

Customer Experience Audit

Capturing the day-to-day context in which people engage with your product or service

- A customer experience audit captures what customers do, think, and use as they set out to achieve a goal that involves your product or service.

- It provides a framework that design teams can use to isolate specific moments of delight, apathy, or frustration before, during, and after an experience.

- Individual moments can be transformed into sources of design team inspiration, from which opportunities for innovation can be identified.

- Qualitative data from interviews and directed story-telling reflects people's social, environmental, and financial realities, underlying beliefs, values, and desires.

- Experience audits can help researchers isolate the areas where they may need to conduct more research as well as any gaps in the service or product offering.

- To keep up with changing social, economic, and technical factors, the audit should be repeated to assess experience with your product over time.

See also   Diary Studies • Directed Storytelling • Experience Sampling Method

As part of every experience design project at the LEGO Group, audits help designers assess whether intended experiences live up to user perceptions and expectations.

034

Data Physicalization

Physical modeling to enable data and relationships to be visualized, experienced, and understood in new ways

- Quantitative and qualitative data need to be synthesized and analyzed, with patterns found and relationships explored.

- Two-dimensional representations of data have dimensions enabling certain mappings and encoding of data.

- Physical modeling of data offers the possibility for other dimensions to be addressed and experienced—including haptic and material properties and even characteristics such as smell.

- Data physicalization can take many forms, from three-dimensional versions of graphs, to intentionally aesthetically focused data sculptures, to complex network diagrams in physical space.

- One important use of data physicalization is as a tool for personal data exploration and reflection, for example, data from self-tracking, quantified self, or digital devices.

Contributed by Dan Lockton

See also Cognitive Mapping • Concept Mapping • Data Visualization

Scenes from a data physicalization workshop, using water-filled balloons of different weights to stretch rubber bands to represent the tension felt by refugees fleeing their homes.

035

Data Visualization

The visual presentation of data to aid the discovery of important relationships among content and to inform meaningful narratives that move people through information

- Wurman's "hat racks," or LATCH—organizes information by location, alphabet, time, category, or hierarchy.

- It is often beneficial to specify a coordinate system that will serve as an anchor for the visualization. Yau outlines coordinate system options as (1) Cartesian (x and y axes), (2) polar (radius and angles), and (3) geographic (latitude and longitude location).

- Scales are used to represent the data accurately and consistently, including linear, categorical, percent, logarithmic, ordinal, and time.

- The emerging organizational structures, coordinate systems, and scales of the data can inform its visual representation.

- Norman's Appropriateness Principle explains the import of having a good fit between form and content.

Contributed by Stacie Rohrbach

See also   Cognitive Mapping • Data Physicalization • Thematic Networks

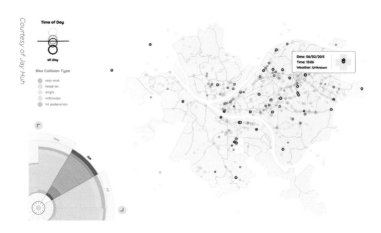

A designer at Carnegie Mellon University leverages Yau's visual cues and Norman's Appropriateness Principle in the representation of bike crash data.

036

Design Charette

A workshop-style technique providing sequential rounds of collaboration and cross-pollination of design ideas

- Designers and non-designers—including project stakeholders, engineers, and users—can participate.

- Participants rapidly generate ideas and rotate through small groups to bring forward the best ideas and move toward superior design concepts.

- A design charette can be used to explore ideas for large-scale design challenges or generate possibilities regarding a very specific interface.

- A moderator should communicate that each round of designs builds off the preferred components identified in the prior cycle.

- The sessions should be low-tech, using basic tools, paper templates, pencils, erasers, and color markers.

- Clarity can be achieved through the active comparison and contrast of many ideas.

See also   Design Workshops • Parallel Prototyping • Participatory Design

pin-up boards

extra supplies

moderator

designers,
stakeholders,
developers,
clients,
customers

Designers, stakeholders, and developers rapidly generate
ideas, rotating through small groups to bring forward and
cross-pollinate the best ideas and move toward superior
design concepts.

037

Design Ethnography

Deep immersive experience and understanding of a user's world for design empathy and insight

- Design ethnography is characterized by descriptive accounts of people in their natural settings, typically using qualitative methods.

- It is focused on a highly contextual, comprehensive, and empathic understanding of users, their lives, their language, their artifacts, and their behaviors.

- In contrast to anthropologist ethnographers who immerse themselves in a culture over extensive periods of time, designers aim to sample behaviors.

- Common methods include experience sampling, diary and photo studies, cultural probes, contextual inquiry, conversational interviews, touchstone tours, and observations.

- Analysis is based on deciphering patterns and themes articulated in a set of design implications in preparation for generative research.

See also   Cultural Probes • Exploratory Research • Participant Observation

Courtesy of Gretchen Mendoza
Photos by Ivette Spradlin

Design ethnography is performed on the mechanic's garage, from a study of understanding how technical knowledge and preventative car care might be supported through design.

038

Design Fiction

The creation and use of real-seeming hypothetical objects, and other media, to explore imaginary narratives and contexts

- The key difference between design fiction and ordinary prototyping is that it is not a matter of exploring functionality, but imaginability.

- In design fiction, the designer typically produces an artifact or film showing part of a story-world as if that world were real. High-fidelity, polished, real-seeming representations of not-yet-possible or counterfactual propositions are a hallmark of the method.

- Design fiction can be connected to the longstanding practice of concept design. It is also related to an array of methodological developments around the exploration of imaginary contexts or longer-range futures.

- This embrace of speculation involves relaxing one or more of the traditional human-centered design constraints of desirability, feasibility, and viability (or desirable, buildable, and profitable) and opens up an enormous range of possibilities.

Contributed by Stuart Candy

See also   How Might We • Prototyping • Transition Design

Players from NASA Jet Propulsion Laboratory use "The Thing from the Future" card game, with contents modified, to scaffold imagination and generate future artifact ideas around possible space missions.

039

Design Workshops

Creative work sessions with participants organized around co-design methods

- Gain the creative trust and input of stakeholders and secure buy-in from team members and clients.

- Workshops can consist of projective techniques such as collage, mapping, or diagramming, to gain an understanding of the user's world.

- There are common in generative research, with participants contributing to ideation through co-design.

- In evaluative sessions, participants collectively review concepts, offer feedback, and contribute insights for design iteration and refinement.

- Workshops may include hands-on training of simple design tools, enabling participants to create mock-ups, sketches, or storyboards, or role-play interactions.

- Plan carefully for a balance of design team facilitators relative to the number of participants, with clearly defined roles.

- These workshops are increasingly used to train interested non-design audiences in the common methods of design research, ideation, thinking, and processes.

See also   Creative Toolkits • Generative Research • Participatory Design

Design workshops engage participants, often non-designers, in intense creative activity centered on assigned problems, as in this workshop on design thinking for business executives.

040

Desirability Testing

Gauging first-impression emotional responses to product and service designs

- Desirability testing explores the affective response that different designs elicit from people based on first impressions.

- Using index cards with positive, neutral, and negative adjectives written on them, participants pick those that describe how they feel about a design or prototype.

- Testing can focus attention on responses from end users, instead of on personal opinions that often leave teams at an impasse.

- When the process is applied repeatedly, the team can begin to compare and cluster the words that are most frequently chosen and visualize the results.

- The method helps focus the design team efforts on shaping the exact emotional response they want people to have while using their products.

- It can be conducted using low-fidelity prototypes or on products already in the public domain as a baseline before the team embarks on a redesign.

See also Triangulation • Usability Testing • Value Opportunity Analysis

	Quality	Appearance	Ease of Use	Motivation	Speed
version 1 (n=14)	Comprehensive (2) Advanced Complex Cutting Edge Integrated	Professional (2) Calm Organized	Usable (2) Accessible Approachable Meaningful Understandable Useful	Compelling Engaging Exciting Fresh Innovative Motivating Novel Stimulating	
version 2 (n=12)	Comprehensive (2) Effective Powerful	Appealing (2) Friendly (2) Professional (2) Business-like Familiar Organized	Useful (5) Usable (4) Clear (2) Collaborative (2) Customizable (2) Flexible (2) Understandable (2) Accessible Controllable Convenient Comfortable Easy to use Meaningful	Relevant (4) Engaging (3) Compelling Creative Fresh Innovative Inspiring Valuable	
version 3 (n=4)	Advanced (2) Comprehensive Creative	Friendly (4) Attractive (2) Organized (2) Clean	Easy to use (6) Useful (5) Clear (3) Accessible (2) Straightforward (2) Collaborative Consistent Helpful Simplistic Usable	Motivating	Fast (3) Time-saving (2) Efficient

Microsoft Product Reaction Cards are a powerful tool for gathering emotional feedback.

041

Diary Studies

Guiding artifacts for convenient expression of personal details about daily life and events

- Diaries are ideal for collecting thoughts, feelings, or behaviors from participants at key moments across time.

- Diaries are designed for portability and ease of use, with an overview of the topic instructions and a sample entry.

- Participants may be requested to document each time they engage in a particular behavior, encounter a product or situation, or have specific interactions.

- Creative page formats can be used to invite text entries, sketches, drawings, photographs, or stickers and multiple-choice responses.

- In rare cases, diaries may be used for usability studies or evaluation, as a means of collecting feedback from users testing products in context over time.

- Using digital diaries, participants record entries on mobile devices or via email or web-based uploads.

See also Cultural Probes • Experience Sampling Method • Photo Studies

(top) Traditional diary study on skin care regimens conducted using pen-and-paper journals. **(bottom)** Digital diary with user photo and text entries describing Christmas shopping experiences.

042

Directed Storytelling

Gathering rich stories of lived experiences using narrative conversational prompts

- Directed storytelling is rooted in narrative inquiry, whereby researchers understand people and document their experiences from personal stories.

- It starts with a prompt by the researcher to the storyteller: "Tell me a story about the last time you . . ."

- Additional guiding questions are posed in terms of who, what, when, where, and how, to keep the storyteller in a comfortable narrative flow.

- Ideas emerging from stories can be clustered using affinity diagramming, looking for consistent patterns and themes within and across experiences.

- Themes that characterize experiences can be modeled into a tangible framework, with maps or diagrams of what is most significant about participant experiences.

- The method may provide subtle reinforcement and validation of existing design directions or identify the need for additional research.

See also   Critical Incident Technique • Interviews • Picture Cards

Guiding questions for directed storytelling might include the following: When and with whom did you interact? What aspects of the environment affected your experience? How did you feel?

043

Drawing

A fundamental tool of design, used to document observations, creatively ideate, and visually communicate

- Drawings occur as a natural function of sketching observations, thoughts, and ideas; concept drawings and renderings; explanatory maps and diagrams; and technical drawings. Drawing can be used to *examine, explore,* and *explain.*

  - **Examining:** Examining observable phenomena and documenting it through drawing can help inspire a thoughtful understanding of the world.

  - **Exploring:** The use of drawing as an exploratory tool references the creative act of iterative ideation, or the generation of multiple concepts through progressive sketching and design development.

  - **Explaining:** Explaining uses drawing as an effective communication tool, conveying ideas to others on the design team, or to clients, users, or stakeholders. Early sketches and concept drawings can be used to convey work in progress. Drawings or storyboards conveying concept scenarios can be used to stimulate discussion and collect feedback.

See also Generative Research • Prototyping • Storyboards

A design research team used drawing to **examine** current laundry behaviors, **explore** various design ideas through iterative sketching, and **explain** proposed design solutions conveyed through product renderings.

044

Elito Method

A method used to ground design arguments in research observations and business directives

- Elito is a rigorous synthesis method designed to help teams bridge the "analysis-synthesis" gap between research and design ideas in a business context.

- Elito brings the multidisciplinary team together after primary and/or secondary research has been conducted.

- Using a spreadsheet and a projector, the team captures its work and thinking in five "Elito entities," which together create "logic line" design arguments:

  - *Observation*: "What did you see, read, or hear?"

  - *Judgment*: "What is your opinion about that observation?"

  - *Value*: "What values are ultimately at work?"

  - *Concept/Sketch*: "What can the design team do to solve this problem?"

  - *Key Metaphor*: "What is the hook or tagline?"

- The spreadsheet captures the team's random, nonlinear thinking to connect arguments, further refine ideas, and organize arguments into observation-based themes.

See also   Cultural Probes • Design Ethnography • Touchstone Tours

After building an Elito spreadsheet based on research observations, each "logic line" is sorted, clustered, and commented upon to analyze, evaluate, and share the work.

045

Empathy Maps

A collaborative template that design teams can populate with user information to gain deeper insights into their customers

- The empathy map canvas consists of several zones: space for identifying goals; zones of questions based on what participants being considered see, say, do, and hear; and questions oriented around what they think and feel, divided into columns of pains and gains.

- Complete the empathy map using these sequential steps:

  1. Beginning with the goals section, determine exactly with whom you are empathizing, and what they hope to accomplish.

  2. Complete the sections according to what you have observed your target users seeing, saying, doing, and hearing. It helps gain a realistic sense of the experiences of your users, to foster empathy.

  3. "Get inside" the heads of the users to determine what thoughts, feelings, and desires are motivating, and what fears, anxieties, or frustrations may be hindering them.

See also   Personas • Scenarios • Swimlanes

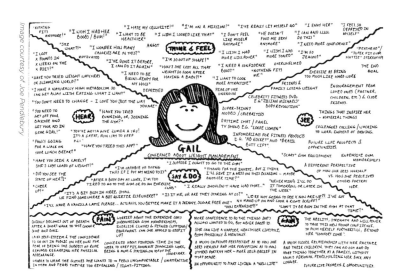

An empathy map visualizing the attitudes and behaviors of a specific user group concerned about weight management.

046

Ergonomic Analysis

An assessment of tools, devices, or environments to optimize fit, safety, and comfort

- Ergonomic analysis is performed to suggest redesign improvements or establish ergonomic criteria for new design.

- The five interrelated criteria commonly used are:

  1. **Size:** Anthropometry is the systematic measurement of people to assess and design tools and systems.

  2. **Strength:** Manual force encompasses finger/hand strength for triggering and gripping and body strength for lifting.

  3. **Reach:** Assesses safe access to operator controls or environmental features and is typically based on fifth percentile females to accommodate most users.

  4. **Clearance:** Assesses effective space within and around machinery and for avoiding environmental obstacles and is commonly based on the 95th percentile male.

  5. **Posture:** Tool and system design should avoid excessive hand deviation or flexion and the reduction of bending and stooping to avoid discomfort, fatigue, and long-term injury.

See also   Evaluative Research • Task Analysis • Usability Testing

Wide jaw opening provides clearance for inserting/removing terminals

High visibility color coding for size

Release mechanism is accessed external to handles for ease of access

Contoured handle with upper and lower touch points to support grip span

Grooved handle overmolding provides comfort, grip stability, and durability

Handle cleat (foot) grips surface for optimal leverage when crimping

An ergonomic analysis of a crimping device hand tool for Thomas & Betts.

047

Evaluative Research

Testing of prototypes, products, or interfaces by users of a system in design development

- Evaluative research gauges human expectations against a designed artifact, determining whether something is useful, usable, and desirable.

- Testing should collect performance measures such as task speed and accuracy and preference measures such as aesthetic and emotional response.

- Research of existing and competing products may be useful in early stage design research, to inform new product development.

- Testing may be conducted in a lab setting or by people using products or prototypes in a real-world context.

- New crowdsourcing opportunities afford online testing by volunteers to assess how users are engaging with prototype interface designs and wireframes.

- Some forms of evaluation research such as cognitive walkthrough and heuristic evaluation use expert evaluators to assess products and interfaces.

See also A/B Testing • Heuristic Evaluation • Think-aloud Protocol

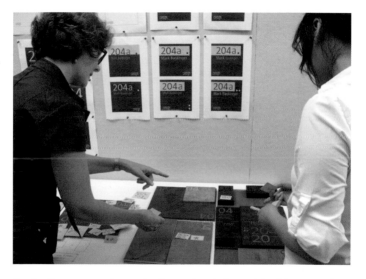

Evaluation research can be formal or informal. In this example, evaluations were invited through a public display of prototypes for a proposed new signage program.

048

Evidence-based Design

Effective design decisions based on credible research and assessed outcomes

- Evidence-based Design (EBD) and Evidence-based Research connect evidence and application, or the applied use of known theories validated by research.

- EBD is applicable across the spectrum of design disciplines for improving service and product touch-points within any environment.

- The primary tenets of EBD are to enter the problem unbiased, employing traditional research methods and factual evidence to influence design decision-making.

- Methods include credible literature reviews and comparative analyses, case studies, and documented post-use evaluations of existing design.

- EBD should also include documented site visits, surveys, interviews, and other means of collecting information.

- Design decisions should be linked to measurable outcomes to justify return on investment, such as reduced infection rates or decreased staff injuries.

See also   Case Studies • Literature Reviews • Secondary Research

This material is based upon work supported by the National Science Foundation under Grant No. IIS-0325047 Courtesy of Peter Scupelli.

Figure 1. An existing surgical suite control desk and schedule board.

Figure 2. Left: Three dimensional sketch of new control desk and schedule board. Right: New floor plan of same. Black circles are control desk workers; white circles are information seekers.

An Evidence-based Design of a surgical suite requires that research informs design decisions, hypotheses are linked to outcomes, design is evaluated, and results are published.

049

Experience Prototyping

Active participation in design through subjective engagement with a prototype system or service, product, or place

- Similar to role-playing and bodystorming, low-fidelity prototypes or props are used to help create a realistic scenario of use and activate felt experiences.

- For exploring and evaluating ideas, design teams can use this method internally and with clients and users.

- Prototypes may include simple props and role-playing or physical and digital prototypes with some level of functionality tested in realistic situations.

- Experience prototyping is effective for persuading key audiences of the values inherent in design concepts, through direct and active engagement.

- A level of functionality allows realistic engagement, yet with a caution that the prototype represents a work in progress and not the final design artifact.

- Advantages are a low cost and addressing situations that will prevent real-life experiences because of inherent risks and dangers or complicating logistics.

See also Bodystorming • Role-playing • Wizard of Oz

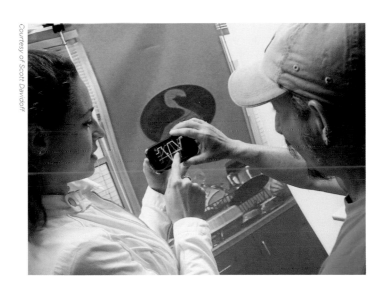

Experience prototypes surround a prototype product or service with a simulated context of use. Here, a user schedules an appointment using a mobile device prototype.

050

Experience Sampling Method

Behaviors, interactions, thoughts, or feelings
self-reported in real time when signaled

- Experience sampling requires participants to document something specific when signaled by a device alarm.

- Before smartphones, participants were signaled by pagers, hence the common nickname of "beeper study."

- Behaviors, interactions, thoughts, or feelings are guided by clear instructions and entered into a pre-established form, often with photos in a diary or journal.

- Technology allows for documenting and sending photos, text, or audio entries through smartphones.

- The method is a form of design ethnography, collecting strategic samples of life in place of in-person immersion by researchers.

- Samples can give the designer a comprehensive picture across time or individuals for any particular design study.

- The method is useful in exploratory and generative phases of design research.

See also   Design Ethnography • Diary Studies • Photo Studies

The "Mappiness" project uses experience sampling to invite respondents to indicate their current feelings and situation when paged, mapping how the environment affects people's happiness.

051

Experiments

Measuring the effect that an action has on a situation, demonstrating a causal relationship

- Cause and effect criteria are met by the cause occurring before the effect of two observable and measurable actions or events and elimination of all other possible causes.

- Through random assignment, experimental group participants are exposed to manipulations of an independent variable, while the control group is not.

- All other conditions are held exactly the same for both groups to rule out the influence of extraneous variables.

- The dependent variable is measured to see if there is a significant difference for those exposed to the manipulation.

- An operational definition defines exactly how the dependent variable is being measured: for example, performance speed or assessment of comfort.

- Quasi-experiments occur when the researcher cannot control the assignment of participants to conditions: for example, comparing pre-existing groups.

See also   A/B Testing • Evaluative Research • Eyetracking

Courtesy of Lester Loschky and Adam Larson, images reproduced with permission from Journal of Vision, © ARVO

In a vision experiment, people were equally good at categorizing the gist of briefly glimpsed scenes using peripheral vision as when seeing the entire image.

052

Exploratory Research

User and product studies intended to forge an empathic knowledge base

- Exploratory research is conducted in the early stages of the design process and set by the planning, scoping, and definition phase.

- The focus is on gaining a solid knowledge base of the design territory and existing artifacts and forging an empathic sense of the people targeted by the design.

- Various diverse yet complementary methods might include contextual inquiry, touchstone tours, surveys, observation, experience sampling, and cultural probes.

- Research is purposefully flexible, encouraging divergence from planned protocols and the inclusion of data from spontaneous interactions and observations.

- Synthesis is critical, but targeted toward inspiration rather than the formal analysis of concrete data.

- Exploratory research culminates in a set of tangible design implications, preparing the groundwork for generative research and concept development.

Contributed by Kelly Nash

See also   Cultural Probes • Design Ethnography • Observation

Exploratory research for a service design project on meat purchasing behaviors included surveys, farm visits, observations, and conversations at meat counters with butchers and consumers.

053

Eyetracking

Technical information documenting where and for how long people are looking when using an interface or interacting with products

- Eye movements tracked during reading or image-gaze tasks are identified for moments of fixation and rapid movements from point to point between fixations.

- Technology traces and documents patterns, generating data for interface and design usability studies.

- Optical methods are used to capture corneal reflections of infrared light on video using sophisticated cameras. Small sensing electrodes precisely detect movements.

- It can help examine printed text and visual materials, engaging with products or product assembly tasks, and navigating environments.

- Data is used to generate heat maps, aggregating data from several participants for a visual analysis of scan patterns and distributed attention.

- Eyetracking should be triangulated with other research methods to understand user motivations, information processing, or comprehension.

See also   Automated Remote Research • Evaluative Research • Experiments

Eyetracking and heat maps are used by eBay to understand where ads could be most effective and useful, helping to shape an advertising strategy.

054

Flexible Modeling

Product or interface configurations generated by users from a component kit of parts

- In industrial design, Velcro modeling presents physical product forms and features sets such as buttons and controls covered in fabric and fasteners for quick configurations.

- In interaction design, interface elements may be presented on paper, card, or in digital form for the users to arrange in a way that makes sense to them.

- For environmental design and space planning, scale model parts or paper templates can be arranged.

- Ambiguous elements may be configured to represent either realistic or ideal "fantasy" artifacts for participants to overlay their own expressions, needs, and desires.

- For analysis, configured artifacts can be sorted by similar characteristics, common user choices, or themes.

- Resulting models can be visually translated into refined designs, using the information provided by participants as guiding inspiration for the designer.

See also   Creative Toolkits • Generative Research • Participatory Design

Flexible modeling presents the participant with a kit of ambiguous parts, in this case components of a backpack, to be configured into preferred arrangements.

055

Fly-on-the-Wall Observation

Unobtrusive observation of people or behaviors, without direct participation or interference

- This method attempts to minimize potential bias or behavioral influences that might result from engagement with users.

- It is appropriate when observing public behaviors or work processes that may be unduly influenced if interrupted or inconvenienced.

- It may reduce the researcher's ability to connect empathically with people and probe further into motivations behind participant behaviors.

- It is generally conducted flexibly, although worksheets or other guiding frameworks may usefully inform observations.

- *Secret outsiders* are distant observers, with a vantage point that removes them from participants to minimize any influence on behaviors.

- *Recognized outsiders* have the nature of their research and role as observer made known to participants, but position themselves in a natural and unobtrusive way.

See also Observation • Shadowing • Unobtrusive Measures

Fly-on-the-Wall Observation is an ideal method for studying public places and activities.

056

Focus Groups

Gauging opinions, feelings, and attitudes about a product, service, marketing campaign, or brand

- The dynamic created by a small group of carefully recruited people, when guided by a skilled moderator, can provide insight into themes, patterns, and trends.

- Focus groups allow participants to openly share experiences, perceptions, wants/needs, and fantasies.

- Design-related inquiries may include:
  - Reviewing processes that take place over time
  - Explanations of what is not desirable about the current state
  - Uncovering the underlying emotions while going through a given process
  - Work-arounds and hacks to improve the process
  - Learning how members establish social capital
  - Understanding constructs and mental models shared by group members

- Pay attention to the logic behind conclusions, stories, metaphors, and analogies, as well as how participants describe their experiences, preferences, and memories.

See also   Directed Storytelling • Laddering • Surveys

A skilled moderator guides a focus group. Sessions are commonly recorded, or stakeholders may observe the session through one-way glass or on-screen.

057

Gap Analysis

An approach aimed at creating effective learning experiences by aligning problems and goals, highlighting design opportunities, and informing the ideation process

- Design opportunities become evident when gaps between current and preferred states are identified.

- It is important to properly identify problems at the onset so that designers can focus on the issues at hand.

- The six levels of Bloom's Revised Taxonomy can help frame goals clearly and effectively: remember, understand, apply, analyze, evaluate, and create.

- Articulating the degree of proficiency that audiences should attain may also be useful. Gery defines levels of proficiency as (1) familiarization, (2) comprehension, (3) conscious effort, (4) conscious action, (5) proficiency, and (6) unconscious competence.

- Dirksen presents five common gaps that bridge current and preferred states: knowledge, skill, motivation or attitude, environmental, and communication.

Contributed by Stacie Rohrbach

See also   How Might We • Importance-Difficulty Matrix • Rose Thorn Bud

Workshop participants work in small groups to define existing problems and brainstorm approaches for bridging the gaps that exist between current and preferred states, which would address existing problems.

058

Generative Research

Engaging users in creative activities to provide rich information for concept development

- Participatory methods include co-design activities as a collaborative process between user and designer.
- Methods may include creative toolkits, design workshops, card sorting, collages, cognitive mapping, diagramming, drawing, and flexible modeling.
- The creation of an artifact around which a participant may talk will act as a trigger for engaged conversation.
- Early phase expressive exercises such as collage enable participants to articulate feelings and desires.
- Later phase exercises consist of constructive methods such as flexible modeling, manipulating design elements oriented toward concept generation.
- Participatory exercises are combined with verbal discussions of work in progress and presentations of creative artifacts emerging from research sessions.
- Focus is on the generation of design concepts and early prototype iterations, ultimately preparing for evaluation, refinement, and production.

See also   Creative Toolkits • Flexible Modeling • Participatory Design

Flexible modeling kits are used by participants in constructive generative research. Here, they are being used to propose desired elements for iPhone apps.

059

Graffiti Walls

An open canvas inviting comments about an environment or system in the context of use

- Large-format paper is temporarily adhered to a wall, with markers readily available for posting open-ended comments.

- The paper may be blank, or a guiding question may be posed to maintain a particular theme.

- The method is useful in environments or situations where it is challenging to collect information through traditional methods such as interview or observation.

- Photos of each graffiti wall should be taken at daily intervals, as the paper may deteriorate or be removed.

- The graffiti wall can be analyzed as a research artifact, for inspiration, comparison, consolidation with walls collected from other locations, and content analysis.

- One limitation is the lack of control and knowledge about who contributed to the information and why.

See also   Exploratory Research • Observation • Unobtrusive Measures

Graffiti walls are ideal for capturing informal opinions about an environment in the context of use, seen here for research on attitudes about public bathrooms.

060

Heuristic Evaluation

An agreed-upon set of usability best practices used to evaluate an interface

- Heuristic evaluation is a usability inspection method that asks evaluators to assess an interface against a set of agreed-upon best practices or usability "rules of thumb."

- Unlike usability tests with actual users, these evaluations enlist team members to inspect and fix baseline usability problems before user testing.

- When heuristics are applied repeatedly during an iterative design process, the principles will become more intuitive and usability problems easier to detect.

- Novices trained on heuristics and evaluators familiar with the subject and usability practices conduct evaluations.

- The method can help detect critical but missing dialogue elements early in the design process, as well as heuristics that are working well.

- When used in the middle phases of the design process, even with low-fidelity prototypes, evaluations can make later usability tests more effective.

See also   Cognitive Walkthrough • Evaluative Research • Prototyping

Aesthetic and
minimalist design

Flexibility and
efficiency of use

Error prevention

A sample of Nielsen's original ten heuristics, adapted and
applied to iPhone apps.

061

Highlight Reels

Short, curated videos that feature key pieces of participant feedback that can be easily shared with stakeholders and teams

- Highlight reels communicate the analysis and synthesis of results from studies using think-aloud protocol.

- Stakeholders can hear directly from participants and experience firsthand what it's like to use the product.

- Make the clips as clean and succinct as possible so that they don't include extra words or words cut in half in the beginning or the end of a clip. At the same time, make sure there is enough context around the feedback so that people who are seeing it for the first time can understand what it's about.

- Good annotations will help you remember what each clip was about, which will save you time when you're assembling the highlight reels.

- The ideal length for a highlight reel is about 3 minutes. Pay attention to the ordering of the individual clips so that they tell a coherent story.

Contributed by Barbora Batokova

See also Think-aloud Protocol • Tree Testing • Usability Testing

The short and to-the-point format of highlight reels is an effective way to share feedback from usability testing. Invite the entire team to have a productive discussion.

062

Horizon Scanning

A set of research approaches for seeking signs of potential change to come in one's operating environment

- The degree of formality and directedness of a scanning activity depends on how specific the knowledge needs of the situation are.

- Scanning is also regarded by many as a fundamental ongoing practice: as events unfold and contexts morph from one day (or year) to the next, the possible, probable, and preferable futures that need to be considered shift too.

- Scanning attention is often guided using a framework like the widely used mnemonic STEEP: Social, Technological, Economic, Environmental, and Political. These lenses prompt the researcher to attend to different facets of change; for when seeking to understand the potential future states of dynamic, complex systems, causes and effects do not stay neatly in disciplinary lanes.

- The basic idea of scanning is to spot and address potential risks and opportunities as early as possible.

Contributed by Stuart Candy

See also   Backcasting • Design Fiction • Transition Design

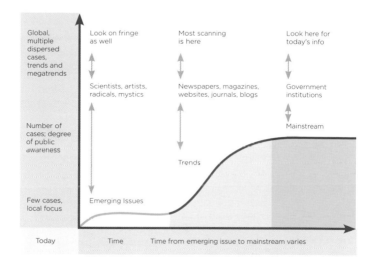

Scanning requires us to venture from the mainstream and the realm of trends, which is all "known" information, to the periphery to find the "new," the emerging signals of change that are the precursor to trends.

Horizon Scanning graph by Maree Conway, Thinking Futures, adapted from Graham Molitor and Wendy Schultz.

063

How Might We

Encouragement of healthy exploration of ideas and potential concepts by starting problem statements with "How might we . . ." often abbreviated as HMW.

- HMW helps to set the stage for brainstorming, and is most often used following exploratory and generative research to advance from insights to potential concepts.

- Common steps of HMW are sequenced as follows:

  1. Specify the material you are exploring.

  2. Reframe the problem or insight into one or more HMW statements, iterating until there is consensus.

  3. Brainstorm solutions in response to the HMW statement, allowing for a range of ideas.

  4. Work to prioritize the ideas, recognizing that this is a first step toward further creative exploration and iterative development of concepts.

- The HMW statement simultaneously narrows and broadens the design direction, taking the team from convergent to divergent thinking.

See also Bull's-Eye Diagramming • Creative Matrix • Kano Analysis

When developing a new concept for an internal site, the team used an HMW statement to solicit additional feedback on wireframes from people who could not attend an in-person session.

064

Image Boards

A collage of pictures, illustrations, or brand imagery to visually communicate aspects of design intent

- Image boards are used to visually convey an essential description of design aesthetics, style, audience, or context.

- Images convey the particular styles, colors, products, brands, and environments associated with the designer's interpretation of a given aesthetic.

- A user-based image board portrays a target audience, conveyed through their clothing, preferred brands, environments, transportation, and social interests.

- An environment-based image board visually shows sample interiors, furniture, lighting, fixtures, and conveys color palettes and atmospheric tone.

- The creation of image boards can serve internally as a consensus artifact for design teams, representing an agreed-upon version of a design aesthetic or context.

- Externally, image boards are powerful tools for communicating design intent to clients, clarifying an aesthetic direction or targeted audience.

See also   Mind Mapping • Stakeholder Maps • Territory Maps

Image boards helped a design team understand the culture and spirit of teenage girls, informing the visual and verbal language for a role-playing game.

065

Importance-Difficulty Matrix

A charting mechanism for teams to reach consensus on design priorities and feature decisions according to value propositions

- The first step in building the matrix is to agree upon the importance of each idea or thematic cluster, arguing for placement on a horizontal spectrum from least to most important.

- When the elements are laid out on this *x*-axis, a vertical *y*-axis is added from least to most difficult. Difficulty here can refer to cost or any other challenge associated with implementation.

- Without changing where ideas have been placed on the horizontal importance dimension, each idea is moved up vertically according to agreed-upon difficulty.

- A four-quadrant grid is superimposed over the plot. Items in the lower left corner are low priority features. Items in the lower right quadrant are high value propositions. Items in the upper left are luxury decisions. Items in the upper right quadrant are reserved for strategic advantage.

See also   Affinity Diagramming • Gap Analysis •
Rose Thorn Bud

Typically it is easier to place issues on the importance (*x*) axis first, then place them on the difficulty (*y*) axis. Highest return on investment issues will be in the lower right.

066

Interviews

Conversation to collect first-hand accounts of experience, opinions, attitudes, and perceptions

- Interviews are best conducted in person to include nuances of personal expression and body language, but may also be conducted by phone or social media.

- Interviews may follow a script of questions or simply have a guiding topic, which allows for flexible detours in conversational form.

- Stakeholder interviews focus on information from specific roles or people who may have a vested interest in the particular inquiry.

- Key informant interviews concentrate on people who have specialized or expert knowledge to contribute.

- Interviews of couples or groups should be moderated so conversations are not dominated by one person.

- Interviews can be more productive when based around artifacts, the inspiration behind methods, personal inventories, and picture cards.

See also   Contextual Inquiry • Questionnaires • Surveys

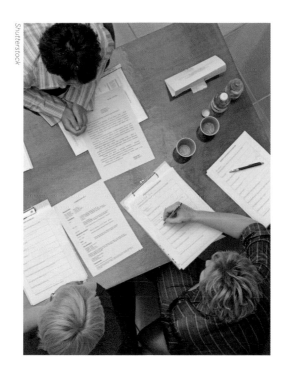

Interviews are a common research method, often used to verify and humanize data collected using complementary methods such as questionnaires and observations.

067

KJ Technique

A silent sort method to help teams work through a problem space and prioritize focus

- The KJ Technique is a consensus-building exercise that helps teams externalize a complicated range of ideas and information.

- It focuses the team on one question and sets everyone to work on the same task at the same time.

- Everyone in the group writes as many problems, data, insights, or opinions as they can think of, in silence.

- Sticky notes are posted simultaneously, opening up the opportunity for a holistic assessment of the problem space rather than competing opinions.

- By providing a framework where everyone silently works together, decisions are made democratically, with little or no opportunities for coercion.

- Working efficiently, a team can organize their notes into an affinity diagram.

See also   Affinity Diagramming • Value Opportunity Analysis • Weighted Matrix

Everyone writes all of their concerns...

...then, notes are sorted in silence...

Using the KJ Technique, team members independently identify their respective concerns and project requirements on sticky notes and then silently cluster similar concerns and challenges.

068

Kano Analysis

Helps determine and prioritize which product attributes are most important to the customer

- By assigning each product attribute to one of five categories, customer values regarding satisfaction can be revealed.

- **Required** (*atari mae* or "quality element") are the baseline features that must be included, such as privacy, safety, and security.

- **Desired** (*ichi gen teki* or "one-dimensional quality element") are attributes that, when included, increase the perceived value of the product.

- **Exciter/Delighter** (*mi ryoku teki* or "attractive quality element") are a source of surprise based on latent customer needs, improving measures of satisfaction.

- **Neutral** (*mu kan shin* or "indifferent quality element") represent features that customers don't have strong feelings for either way.

- **Anti-feature** (*gyaku* or "reverse quality element") attributes provide insight into what you should leave out of a product.

See also   Desirability Testing • Surveys • Value Opportunity Analysis

The Kano Analysis can help you make informed decisions about which product features to improve first or in what order to add features.

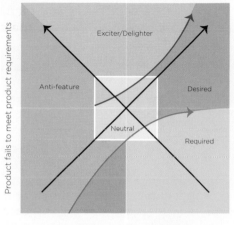

Question 1: If product attribute is present, the customer feels...

		Satisfied	Neutral	Dissatisfied
Question 2: If product attribute is absent, the customer feels...	Satisfied	Questionable	Anti-feature	Anti-feature
	Neutral	Exciter/ Delighter	Neutral	Anti-feature
	Dissatisfied	Desired	Required	Questionable

069

Key Performance Indicators (KPIs)

Measurements of how well you are doing against quantifiable, widely accepted business goals

- KPIs measure where you were yesterday and where you are today, in relationship to where you are trying to go in terms of some predefined business objective.

- Each KPI is a measurement derived from an individual's interaction with your product or service.

- KPIs are great for quantifying behavior or value metrics (e.g., the ratio of people who abandon their shopping cart versus those who complete the sale).

- As an action-oriented measure, KPIs can help:

  - Recognize, prioritize, and react as issues occur

  - Meaningfully summarize and compare data and use it to your advantage

  - Document a business case for change

  - Foster an ongoing organizational understanding of how people respond to your product or service

- The KPI reporting process needs to be ongoing and frequent enough so that fluctuations can be immediately course-corrected.

See also   Site Search Analytics • Web Analytics

	Senior Strategists	Tactical Team Members
Content Sites	• Average page views per visit • Average cost per visit • Average revenue per visit • % high, med, low frequency visitors	• % of visitors using search • % high, med, low click depth visits • Landing page bounce rate • RSS/email subscription conversion rate
Marketing Sites	• Lead generation conversion rate • Average cost per lead generated • Average (estimated) revenue per visit • Average cost per lead generated	• Landing page bounce rate • Average searches per visit • % zero yield searches • Lead generation rate for campaigns
Customer Service Sites	• Average time to respond to email inquiries • % high, low customer satisfaction • % new and returning customers	• % high, medium, low click depth visits • % zero yield searches • Form completion rates • Download completion rates
Online Retailers	• Order conversion rate • Buyer conversion rate • Average revenue per visit • Average cost per conversion • % high, low satisfaction customers	• Search to purchase conversion rate • % of low recency visitors • Cart and checkout completion rate • Order conversion rate by campaign type • Zero yield searches

This shows the recommended KPIs for four popular business models and which internal team should monitor them.

070

Laddering

An interviewing technique that reveals connections between a product's characteristics and personal values

- Laddering builds on Means–End Theory, which posits that people make purchasing decisions based on consequences afforded by using the product.

- It connects a product's obvious physical characteristics to values by repeatedly asking "Why" questions.

- As the conversation builds on itself to reveal what a person values, the "ladder" is constructed that connects product attributes to the consequences and to the individual's values.

- Consequences are the benefit or the impact that the product has on a person and reveal another layer about what is important.

- Values expose the root cause behind why a product resonates profoundly with a person.

- Seven values are often the motivation behind purchasing behavior: self-esteem, accomplishment, belonging, self-fulfillment, family, satisfaction, and security.

See also   Interviews • Triading • Value Opportunity Analysis

Laddering is used to reveal the connection between a product's obvious physical characteristics and the deeper personal values that it reinforces in a customer's life.

071

Literature Reviews

The written collection and synthesis of research on a given topic

- Literature reviews are intended to distill information from published sources, capturing the essence of previous research or projects to inform the current project.

- Strategies for organizing may be categorical, chrono-logical, thematic, or methodological.

- Internet resources have expedited searches, but judgment is needed to ensure relevance and credibility of sources.

- References may include books, chapters, journal and magazine articles, theses and dissertations, corporate and academic websites and blogs, and past design projects.

- The guiding factor in selecting literature should be relevance, clearly suggesting how it informed the design investigation.

- Literature reviews should be accurately referenced using a consistent bibliographic style.

See also Evidence-based Design • Secondary Research • Unobtrusive Measures

Extracting salient information from precedent research and projects through comprehensive literature reviews is a critical step in laying the foundation and contextualizing the design inquiry.

072

The Love Letter & the Breakup Letter

Writing to express sentiments to a personified product or service

- *The Love Letter* conveys what people feel during moments of connection with a product, including delight, infatuation, and loyalty.

- *The Breakup Letter* provides insight about how, when, and where a relationship with a product turned sour, to understand why people abandon a product.

- Both exercises are great techniques to use in a group dynamic, including design workshops, group interviews, and icebreaker sessions.

- Ask participants to spend no more than ten minutes on a letter and then volunteers can read theirs aloud.

- The physical letters are important research artifacts, while video can capture participant expressions and voices.

- Methods like the Love Letter and the Breakup Letter build our empathic knowledge base of how people experience and personify designs.

See also   Design Workshops • Desirability Testing • Value Opportunity Analysis

The Love Letter and Breakup Letter allow participants to express their love or disappointment to a product or service with a handwritten letter.

073

Mental Model Diagrams

A framework aligning task behaviors, beliefs, and emotions with product and service features

- Mental model diagrams can help you articulate root causes behind behaviors and develop solutions that deeply resonate with people.

- Diverse groups identified for study are called task-based audience segments, each usually comprised of at least four people.

- Diagrams are built from the bottom up, using singularly focused behaviors, beliefs, and emotions derived from interviews or diary studies.

- The top half of the diagram represents the behaviors, beliefs, and emotions people have as they set out to accomplish a task.

- The bottom half of the diagram represents the features, product, and service offering.

- The goal is to help teams make appropriate product development strategies that align with how people already approach problem solving in their daily lives.

See also   Diary Studies • Interviews • Task Analysis

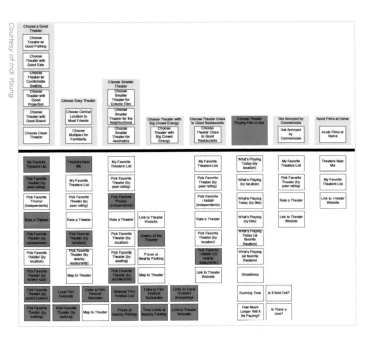

The top half of the diagram represents behaviors, beliefs, or emotions. The bottom half represents the features, services, or products available in your current offering.

074

Metaphors

A method to investigate how people understand concepts, help them understand in new ways, and generate new ideas

- A metaphor is "a device for seeing something in terms of something else. It brings out the thisness of a that or the thatness of a this."

- Interaction and product design often use metaphors to introduce people to new ways of doing things, by relating them to familiar ideas.

- Designers can use a process of eliciting the metaphors that people might be—consciously or unconsciously—using to imagine or understand the systems around them, or complex ideas.

- Participatory drawing methods, image collages or mood boards, or even constructing physical models can all help as projective methods to reveal the underlying metaphors, associations, and mental models that people use to make meaning around particular topics or ideas. Analysis of these metaphors can uncover their effects and implications.

Contributed by Dan Lockton

See also   Creative Toolkits • Generative Research • Picture Cards

New Metaphors is a workshop method where participants juxtapose seemingly unrelated cards to generate novel metaphors for hard-to-visualize phenomena (e.g., Plant Growth as a metaphor for Feeling Overwhelmed).

075

Mind Mapping

A visual thinking tool to organize and understand the complexities of a problem space

- Mind mapping can help generate ideas and develop concepts using the following steps:

  1. Identify a themed focus question to draw in the center.

  2. Label extensions with simple verb-noun pairs or noun clusters.

  3. Connect primary and secondary connections with lines to create meaning.

  4. Continue free associations until all relevant information is represented.

  5. Before declaring the map complete, reflect for a while.

- The map provides a nonlinear means of externalizing the information in our heads so that we can interpret, consolidate, communicate, store, and retrieve it.

- The map allows us to summarize and test assumptions, make and break connections, and consider alternatives while we shape data into themes and patterns.

See also   Brainstorm Graphic Organizers • Collage • Concept Mapping

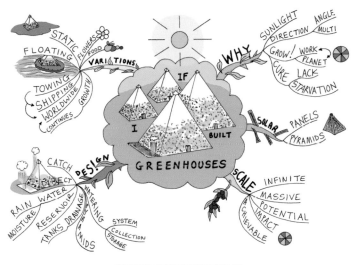

© Paul Foreman http://www.mindmapinspiration.com

Mind mapping allows us to simultaneously identify the subject of the map, relationships between the components, and understand the relative importance of the information represented.

076

Observation

Attentive looking and systematic recording of people, artifacts, environments, events, behaviors, and interactions

- Semi-structured observation typically describes ethno-graphic methods in the exploratory phase of design.

- Ethnographic observations should be flexible, yet systematic, careful, and well documented with notes, sketches, photographs, or video.

- Semi-structured observations are typically synthesized for guiding design inspiration, but content analysis may be performed to uncover themes or patterns.

- Structured, or systematic observation, is formalized by pre-structure utilizing worksheets to track time intervals, behavioral categories, or counted successes and errors.

- If sample sizes are large enough, results can be quantified for analysis otherwise, it is common to look for patterns or trends across observations.

- Observations should differentiate between factual behaviors witnessed and inferences, speculating the meaning and motivations behind actions.

See also AEIOU • Fly-on-the-Wall Observation • Participant Observation

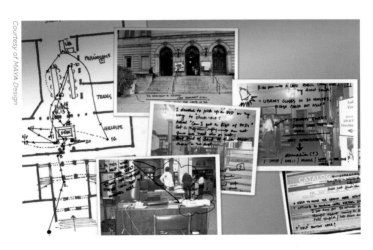

Documented contextual observations from a customer-centered study of the library experience to inform redesign.

077

Parallel Prototyping

Simultaneously exploring multiple design ideas before selecting one approach

- Parallel prototyping can help teams from fixating on a design direction too early, improve the nature of design critiques, and lead to more effective design results.

- Designers quickly and independently create a divergent range of low-fidelity prototypes and then submit designs to testing by end users or to heuristic evaluation by experts.

- Evaluations help designers to thoughtfully consider how people react to individual elements of the design and which accomplish the project's intended goals.

- The method shifts focus from the designer onto the design, promoting a safe environment where critiques are more engaging, less personal, and less stressful.

- The method promotes team collaboration and builds rapport, as designers will often merge and refine others' concepts into their subsequent designs.

See also Design Charette • Prototyping • Research Through Design

By simultaneously designing and testing multiple approaches, there is a better chance that the final design will represent the best qualities of all design options.

078

Participant Observation

Immersive membership in an activity, context, culture, or subculture

- A participant observation (PO) researcher forms deep connections and empathy by experiencing events in the same way as the people they are studying.

- PO is a foundational method of anthropology, adapted for design use through time-limited engagements.

- Systematic observation and recording are critical to document physical aspects of the environment, behaviors, interactions, language, motivations, and perceptions of the participants.

- Marginal participants blend into an environment as natural observers of an activity or event.

- Full participants take on a membership role or may already occupy a role that allows for full participation.

- Participant observers need to stay vigilant to retain some measure of objectivity and to avoid undue influence on member behaviors.

See also   Design Ethnography • Fly-on-the-Wall Observation • Observation

Marginal participant observation of transit riders for a service design project on "commutenity," promoting community and reinforcing positive behaviors among bus riders.

079

Participatory Action Research

A cyclical, collaborative process that seeks to intentionally change members of the inquiry

- The mission is to change the community, or policies under study, differentiated from objective methods that seek only to describe, understand, and explain.

- With an overtone of empowerment, emancipation, and activism, the approach has been popular in education, feminist research, and social justice.

- The process is dynamic and cyclical in its sequence of planning, taking action, observing, evaluating, and critical reflection.

- Specific research methods tend to be flexible, qualitative, and ethnographic, including traditional observations, participant observation, and interviews.

- New movements in social design suggest a natural affiliation with participatory methods, including collaborative design workshops and creative toolkits.

- It is a powerful process when aligned with issues identified by a community, inspiring action to be applied directly to problems.

See also   Case Studies • Civic Design & Policy • Participatory Design

In research designing a health literacy game, participants described undergoing improved self-image, better physical and psychological well-being, and positive reinforcement from friends and family.

080

Participatory Design

A human-centered approach advocating co-design engagement with users and stakeholders

- Participatory design has its roots in Scandinavia in the 1970s, where computer professionals worked with unions to integrate new technology into the workplace.

- Participatory design encompasses several methods, unified by face-to-face contact in activity-based co-design engagements.

- Methods include cultural probes, diary studies, photo studies, collage, flexible modeling, role-playing, creative toolkits, and design workshops.

- Participatory design respects the creative insight of participants to inspire and help guide the design process and to respond to design outcomes.

- A framework of participatory design describes the form of method or technique (making, telling, and enacting) and purpose.

- Purposes are probing participants for self-discovery, priming for further participation, understanding current experience, and generation of future scenarios and concepts.

See also   Creative Toolkits • Design Workshops • Generative Research

In this participatory design project on appliance design for the aging population, participants use creative toolkits for design input and offer feedback on prototypes.

081

Personal Inventories

Representative collections of artifacts selected by
the participant for the designer-researcher

- A personal inventory allows the designer to see and
  understand the relevance of objects in a user's life in
  order to inspire design themes and insight.

- It is most commonly solicited through paired methods
  such as guided tours, contextual interviews, and photo
  and diary studies.

- As a component of touchstone tours, participants talk
  about the things they own as they walk the researcher
  through their home or other environment.

- As an element of photo studies, participants document
  the objects of meaning, often with companion notations.

- Interviews probe for object meaning, the role in a
  participant's life, acquisition, use, placement, and how
  they might feel if the object were lost or damaged.

- Personal inventories may focus on certain types of
  objects, but are more commonly driven by the
  participant, who identifies items of significance.

Contributed by Will Odom

See also   Artifact Analysis • Diary Studies • Touchstone Tours

Personal inventories can reveal the significance of objects, but may rely on the designer to extract insight about the user and context for design inquiry.

082

Personas

Representative human profiles based on archetypal descriptions of users from research

- Personas are crafted from information collected from real users through sound field research and captures common behaviors in meaningful and relatable profiles.

- Personas are useful in humanizing design focus, testing scenarios, and aiding in design communication.

- Human descriptions facilitate easy empathy and communication, while distinctions create useful targets for responsible design.

- Affinity diagramming or other methods can be used to cluster similarities across users to form archetypes.

- Personas are typically page-length descriptions, with a name, a photo, and a story describing key aspects of life, goals, and behaviors.

- Personas are used as a lasting human reference by teams throughout all phases of the project.

- Provide a persuasive human reference when communicating research summaries and scenarios to clients.

See also   Scenarios • Swimlanes • User Journey Maps

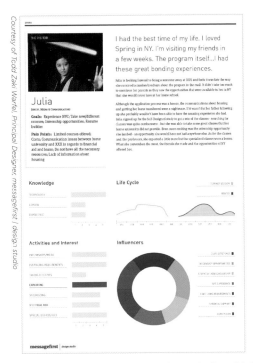

This is a persona of a college student. The majority of information about the persona is visually illustrated to reflect her knowledge, activities and interests, influencers, and backstory.

083

Photo Studies

Self-documentation of a participant's life and interactions

- Photo studies are common in exploratory research as a method for understanding the world of users, particularly when engaging in territory unfamiliar to the designer.

- To initiate a photo study, participants are provided with a camera or instructed how their own cameras are to be used for the purposes of the research.

- Participants are given general instructions on what to document, or they may be instructed to take images at certain times or when feeling a particular way.

- Photo studies are most often used as a complement to other methods: for example, diary studies or the experience sampling method.

- The designer may rely solely on the photographs and participant notes for synthesis or have the participant explain or sort their photos.

- Patterns and themes might emerge within several photos from multiple participants.

See also   Cultural Probes • Diary Studies • Experience Sampling Method

Collected photos from a crowdsourced photo study on energy use reveal a diverse range of interpretations on the subject matter for design consideration.

084

Picture Cards

Cards with images and words that help people think about and share true experiences

- In a session, participants recall an experience, using the cards to support memories and evoke conversation.

- Picture cards stem from activity theory, which asserts, "the human mind is the product of our interaction with people and artifacts in the context of everyday activity."

- Cards are created with images and caption text relevant to the research inquiry, but connected to the personal accounts of participant lives.

- Card sets should account for current and future product and service experiences and include blank cards for details that might emerge during sessions.

- The method should be used flexibly, adding, subtracting, and editing picture cards in pretesting prior to field use and even between research sessions.

- The cards can be used for sorting current products and services used and "sketching" future scenarios, which are laid out as a story unfolds.

See also   Directed Storytelling • Interviews • Touchstone Tours

In a picture card session, cards are sorted by participants and used to guide storytelling of past experiences and the sketching of future scenarios.

085

Prototyping

The tangible creation of artifacts, at various levels of resolution, for development and testing of ideas

- Prototypes are essential for early and iterative concept testing by the design team, clients, and potential users.

- Low-fidelity prototyping is common throughout early ideation processes in all design disciplines, appearing as concept sketches, storyboards, or sketch models.

- A common method of low-fidelity prototyping in interface and software design is paper prototyping, with printed pages representing interface screens.

- In graphic design, the "comp" serves as a low-fidelity prototype, presenting a mocked-up version of a proposed printed piece, usually for client review.

- In industrial design, low-fidelity prototypes may be sketch models intended for iterative design review or as proof of concept models to test form and scale.

- High-fidelity prototypes represent the appearance of the final product in look and feel and basic functionality, through interactive computer or physical models.

See also   Experience Prototyping • Research Through Design • Storyboards

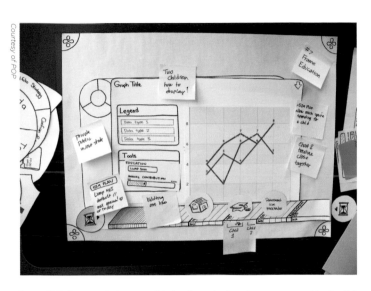

Low-fidelity prototypes of interface behaviors are used to build consensus and understanding among project team members and clients.

086

Questionnaires

Self-reported information about thoughts, feelings, perceptions, behaviors, or attitudes

- Questionnaires are one of the primary tools used to collect survey information, the other being interviews.

- Questionnaires are simple to produce and administer, but careful attention should be paid to question wording and response options, sequencing, and length.

- Factors in securing a good response rate in both print and digital questionnaires include appearance, clarity, instructions, arrangement, design, and layout.

- Open-ended questions provide opportunity for depth of response, whereas closed-ended questions are easier to numerically analyze and communicate.

- To maintain question neutrality while also gaining an indication of strength of response, Likert scale questions are highly recommended.

- They are commonly triangulated with other methods, such as observation, to supplement the data with personal insights and verify self-reported behaviors.

See also   Interviews • Semantic Differential • Surveys

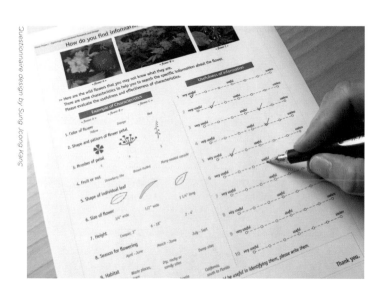

Questionnaires can be used as a component of various forms of research: for example, as part of a diary study or an element of product evaluation.

087

Rapid Iterative Testing & Evaluation (RITE)

A powerful formative usability inspection method that identifies early interface problems

- RITE is a rigorous method used to evaluate and identify interface problems, quickly fix them, and then empirically verify the efficacy of the fixes.

- RITE explores user behavior insights relative to design direction as opposed to summative goals, which measure usability issues.

- Prototypes are changed as soon as problems are identified and the team agrees to a solution, and the fix is then retested with more participants.

- Scheduled tests continue after each design change until there is a string of successes with no failures.

- Domain knowledge can help observers prioritize fixes based on their judgment of true problems versus what is an artifact of a particular participant.

- RITE begins when you have a low-fidelity prototype to test, in order to fix issues before time and resources are spent producing a high-fidelity prototype.

See also Prototyping • Think-aloud Protocol • Usability Testing

AN EXAMPLE RITE TEST CYCLE

TEST **1**

Test 1 succeeds. You need 2 more successful tests.

TEST **2**

Test 2 fails. After fixing the issues, you reset your counter for 3 more successful tests.

TEST **3**

Tests 3 succeeds. You need 2 more successful tests.

TEST **4**

Test 4 succeeds. If test 5 is unsuccessful, reset your counter. If it succeeds, the design succeeds!

Totals: 5 participants
2 revised prototypes

An example test cycle using the RITE method.

088

Remote Moderated Research

Remotely observing users completing tasks on their own devices in context

- A participant completes tasks while thinking out loud while software allows a remote researcher and observers to review behaviors and ask questions.

- Remote moderated research can reveal deep insights into contexts of use that cannot be replicated in a controlled lab environment.

- The method exposes rich, qualitative data about a participant's native computer and possibly his or her physical environment.

- With "live recruiting," participants can be intercepted when they begin a process, and research can be initiated immediately upon their consent.

- Live recruiting allows the research team to observe behavior in a task that the participant has selected as important and relevant as opposed to one assigned.

See also   Stakeholder Walkthrough • Time-aware Research • Usability Testing

Observers

The participant

The researcher

As a participant completes tasks while thinking out loud, screen-sharing software allows a remote researcher and observers to review behaviors and ask questions.

089

Research Through Design

Utilizing the design process as a reflective research activity to enhance design practices

- Research through design examines the tools and processes of design thinking and making within the design project, bridging theory and building knowledge.

- It is constituted by the design process itself, including the critical act of recording and communicating the steps, experiments, and iterations of design.

- Designers utilize their work, including sketches, drawings, models, and prototypes to interrogate ideas, test hypotheses, and pose new questions.

- As an approach to interaction design, this method integrates models and theories with technical knowledge in the design process.

- Designers who conduct their research through creative, critically reflective practice may at once be responding to a design brief and a set of larger questions.

- Documentation is critical to contextualize and communicate design action, advance scholarship, and enhance the inventory of design resources.

See also   Case Studies • Evidence-based Design • Prototyping

These form studies embody an inquiry into materials, surfaces, volumes, and edges, informing research and teaching in the experimentation and generation of form.

090

Role-playing

Acting the role of the user in realistic scenarios to present empathic design opportunities

- Role-playing is usually guided by describing a general situation or suggestions for actions to be performed, tasks to be accomplished, or goals to be reached.

- Members of the design team have to be willing to play and improvise, yet be cautious to avoid exchanges that can lead to hurtful or upsetting words or actions.

- Debriefing after role-playing is critical to make sense of what occurred and to assess genuine feelings that may have resulted from the session.

- Role-playing is difficult to document by the actors involved, so it is useful to have other team members record the sessions using photos and notes or video.

- Role-playing is useful when direct observation is not feasible or ethical: for example, for personally sensitive situations or where access to the users is restricted.

See also   Bodystorming • Experience Prototyping • Simulations

Members of design teams engaged in role-playing have to be willing and realistic participants. Here, designers are enthusiastically role-playing services for parents with young children.

091

Rose Thorn Bud

A method used to identify elements of a design system that are working well, working poorly, and emerging as possibilities yet to be explored

- Elements of a designed system are identified as roses if they are largely positive and working well as is. Elements that need to be addressed because of negative factors or aspects that are working poorly are flagged as thorns. Aspects that have yet to be fully explored for their potential but that show signs of promise are considered buds.

- In a typical scenario, features are noted by hand on color-coded sticky notes and clustered into the three categories.

- The method can also be expanded for participatory engagement with users or stakeholders of a product, system, or service. In this case, research participants would identify roses, thorns, and buds from the first-person user or stakeholder point of view. Members of the design team would serve as facilitators and turn the insights gained into actionable design implications.

See also   Affinity Diagramming • Gap Analysis • Importance-difficulty Matrix

Conducting a Rose Thorn Bud helped participants understand the value of using an accessible tool with "just enough structure" to ensure balanced inquiry and a breadth of analysis.

092

Scenarios

A narrative exploring the future use of a product from a user's point of view

- A scenario is a believable narrative, usually set in the future, of a person's experience as he or she engages with a product or a service.

- By making design ideas explicit and concrete, the design team can empathetically envision the future ways in which a product is likely to be used.

- The scenario should focus efforts on building culturally meaningful artifacts that augment actual human activity, rather than designing toward technical requirements.

- Scenarios bring personas to life. Both deliverables therefore reinforce the value of the other.

- Scenarios should range from baseline, status quo to high-stress situations with less-than-optimal conditions.

- Scenarios can be written to follow a traditional story arc, with a trigger event, scene, and preconditions, and task resolution with technology that assists and delights.

See also   Design Fiction • Personas • Speed Dating

A goal-oriented scenario with a customer persona, showing key interactions and barriers to a successful library experience.

093

Secondary Research

Information collected and synthesized from
existing data and sources

- Secondary research establishes what has been done
  and what hasn't, identifying opportunity gaps to help
  suggest a research direction and methods.

- It is sometimes referred to as desk research, in
  contrast to primary research conducted as fieldwork
  or empirical research.

- Sources may include books, research papers, journal
  articles, and conference papers, records and statistics,
  or any number of other archives.

- In design, research might include precedent projects,
  products or documented case studies, photographs,
  maps, diagrams, and other visual support records.

- It is traditionally summarized in systematic reviews or
  literature reviews, with full citations of sources.

- In design, secondary research can also be collected
  into visual summaries or blogs, for shared viewing,
  sorting, synthesis, and the crafting of narratives.

See also   Case Studies • Literature Reviews •
Unobtrusive Measures

The WorldCat database allows users to search the collections and services of more than 10,000 libraries worldwide, including the option to select specific media types.

094

Semantic Differential

A linguistic tool designed to measure people's attitudes toward a topic, event, object, or activity

- The semantic differential asks respondents to indicate where on a continuum of antonyms a concept is best described (e.g., pleasant–unpleasant).

- The three dimensions to classify concepts are evaluation (e.g., valuable–worthless), potency (e.g., strong–weak), and activity (e.g., active–passive).

- Concepts should be chosen based on research objectives and should be meaningful to respondents.

- Poles should be randomized so that negative and positive connotations don't always fall on the same side.

- A seven-point scale is preferred because it provides a neutral midpoint, which could indicate apathy, indecisiveness, or social relevance.

- How various concepts are mapped in a semantic space reflect their differences in connotative meaning.

See also Laddering • Questionnaires • Surveys

Please rate this human on the adjective scales below.

		1	2	3	4	5	6	7
1=Awful	7=Nice	○	○	○	○	○	○	○
1=Machinelike	7=Humanlike	○	○	○	○	○	○	○
1=Artificial	7=Lifelike	○	○	○	○	○	○	○
1=Unpleasant	7=Pleasant	○	○	○	○	○	○	○
1=Fake	7=Natural	○	○	○	○	○	○	○
1=Unfriendly	7=Friendly	○	○	○	○	○	○	○
1=Unconscious	7=Conscious	○	○	○	○	○	○	○
1=Unkind	7=Kind	○	○	○	○	○	○	○

Please rate this human on the adjective scales below.

		1	2	3	4	5	6	7
1=Awful	7=Nice	○	○	○	○	○	○	○
1=Machinelike	7=Humanlike	○	○	○	○	○	○	○
1=Artificial	7=Lifelike	○	○	○	○	○	○	○
1=Unpleasant	7=Pleasant	○	○	○	○	○	○	○
1=Fake	7=Natural	○	○	○	○	○	○	○
1=Unfriendly	7=Friendly	○	○	○	○	○	○	○
1=Unconscious	7=Conscious	○	○	○	○	○	○	○
1=Unkind	7=Kind	○	○	○	○	○	○	○

Eight semantic differential scales were used to investigate the degree to which a person's cultural background influences one's perception of a robot's anthropomorphism and likeability.

095

Service Blueprint

A visual representation allowing the designer and co-creators to share a bird's-eye view of an existing or proposed service

- There are three main components to the Service Blueprint: **frontstage** (the experience of the service), **backstage** (inside the organization), and **infrastructure** (technology and resources needed for the service to exist).

- Frontstage aims to map and understand the different dynamics in which the user of the service and stakeholders in direct contact with him/her are involved.

- Backstage aims to map and understand interactions and exchanges within the team, organization, or institution that provides the service.

- Mapping infrastructure that enables the service helps to understand how a preferred avenue of production or resource management can be put into place to pinpoint areas of tension between intangible actors and tangible materials to improve the users' service experience.

Contributed by Sofía Bosch Gómez and Marysol Ortega Pallanez

See also   Business Origami • Service Design • Stakeholder Maps

Designers condense an overview of a service into a single visual blueprint that allows them to understand the full set of dynamics that regulate it.

		PREPARATION						RECEPTION			
WEEKS	1	2	3	4	5	6	7	8	9	10
FRONTSTAGE — CUSTOMER ACTIONS		Sends email for onboarding	Mentor looks for PD or recruitment	Accepts the invite	Budget catering for mentors	Pick up cash	Look for mentee	Mentor receives invitation to graduation	Feedback	Receives and fills feedback form
MEDIA TOUCHPOINTS		Video call / Face to face		calendar						
STAFF ACTIONS		Recruit mentors		Give insights	Information session	Confirm budget	Turn in letter of responsibility	Mentor & mentor are given a tour	Guidelines for expected feedback	Graduation invitation	Send compilations
BACKSTAGE — BACKSTAGE STAFF	Discussion & deliberation / Volunteer List	Recruitment Process / Register in PD DB	Calendarize information session / Get room	Read and update material		Email Finances	Print information	Inform mentor	Send evaluation form	Graduation logistics	Organize information in shared document
SUPPORT PROCESS	Excel / Video call Concertation	Mail Messages	Room in calendar	Slides / Technical equipment		Finances: have cash ready	Finances		Digital form + document		

A service analyzed through different stakeholders under the lenses of frontstage and backstage according to the service's visibility from the user's perspective, bridging the infrastructure of the service.

Service Blueprint adapted by Marysol Ortega Pallanez and Sofía Bosch Gómez from original by Denisse Gutiérrez, Diana Arvayo, and Miguel Medina

096

Service Design

A contextual and temporal systems approach for understanding, envisioning, planning, and regulating services by engaging in co-creative processes with stakeholders

- A systems perspective allows designers to tackle the complexity of services by seeing them as a series of interconnected touchpoints—stakeholders, artifacts, technologies, environments, interactions, and processes—with a human-centered mindset.

- Service design highlights the connections between the service and the organization offering it.

- It recognizes that services manifest across time; therefore, we cannot predict in detail how they will unfold. As a result, designers go through processes of modeling and mapping the conditions that might influence the service.

- It tackles the invisible nature of services by using our ability to visualize and make ideas tangible, to allow people to explore future experiences.

Contributed by Sofía Bosch Gómez and Marysol Ortega Pallanez

See also   Civic Design & Policy • Participatory Design • Service Blueprint

The Pop Up
Axon Diagram

Interactive Panels

Spectacle Liaison

Photo Opportunity

The Web App

A Tool for Building Experiences
Answer a simple quiz to find a music centric packaged experience tailored to you

Physical Invitation
Experience

You are Invited
Users can select to receive a physical invitation that serves as a passport to their experience

Three primary touchpoints of a personalized package experience for a cultural event include a pop-up exhibition with interactive panels, a web app, and a physical invitation.

097

Shadowing

An observational method tracking someone closely through his or her daily routines

- Observing a participant's activities and decision patterns allows researchers to gather insights through firsthand, real-time exposure.

- Observations should be well documented, with photographs, detailed notes and sketches, or audio.

- Ideally, several team members will complete shadowing exercises across representative users, to begin crafting a general picture of patterns.

- Cooperation is necessary and a respectful distance should be maintained to avoid interruption to natural routines or behavior change as a result of being observed.

- Typically, interactions with the person being shadowed are kept to a minimum, asking pertinent questions about behaviors after the shadowing session.

- Subtle covert shadowing may be utilized to observe public behaviors: for example, following students on campus to determine common pathways.

See also Behavioral Mapping • Fly-on-the-Wall Observation • Touchstone Tours

In a study of the relationship between food providers and consumers in creating sustainable food communities, grocery shoppers were shadowed, asked about their decisions, and photographed.

098

Simulations

Deep approximations of human or environmental conditions

- Effective simulations forge a tangible, immersive sense of real-life user experience to influence design sensitivity and decisions.

- Simulated real-world conditions can provide empathic emotional experiences or test functional interactions like response time and decision-making.

- These exercises have been used in military, aircraft and NASA training, driving simulators, and virtual worlds.

- In design, exercises might approximate the limitations experienced by people with physical disabilities, brain injuries, or age-related sense and cognition deficits.

- Low-tech simulations can utilize wheelchairs, manipulated glasses lenses, or blindfolds to empathically experience restricted mobility or visual impairment.

- Designers are involved in the creation of simulated environments such as video games, virtual or augmented reality, physical spaces, and artifacts.

See also   Bodystorming • Experience Prototyping • Role-playing

Researchers perform tasks wearing the "Age Gain Now Empathy System" (AGNES), developed in the MIT AgeLab to simulate the dexterity, mobility, strength, and balance of a 74-year-old.

099

Site Search Analytics

Reporting and analyzing user queries submitted as search criteria on a site

- Analyzing words and phrases entered into a search provides insight into what people are looking for in order to evaluate how well content meets those needs.

- Site search analytics can bolster customer retention, satisfaction, and conversion rates, aligning user-centered activity to measurable business goals.

- For qualitative research, understanding user intent and the information people want from your site can help you evaluate and improve the quality of the search results.

- For quantitative data, a Zipf distribution represents the statistical majority of search terms within a given time frame, pinpointing which should be optimized.

- If you are in "Launch & Monitor" phase, relate site search performance metrics to your organization's existing Key Performance Indicators (KPIs).

- The data revealed by site search analytics can help you monitor and improve your application's overall performance.

See also   Content Inventory & Audit •
Key Performance Indicators • Web Analytics

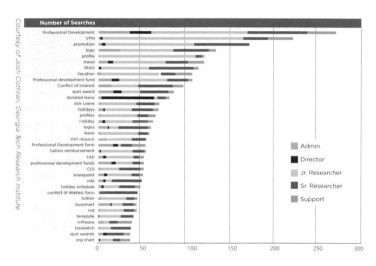

Here is an example of a typical site search analytics Zipf distribution, where a small number of search terms represent the most popular searches.

100

Speed Dating

The rapid review of multiple design concepts by multiple users in quick succession

- Speed dating introduces people to design ideas via storyboards and simulated environments before expensive technical prototypes are built by using the following process:

  - Conduct contextual field research via methods such as interviews, role-playing, artifact analysis, directed storytelling, diary studies, and cultural probes.

  - Create storyboards to elicit an emotional, empathic reaction to relatable characters in convincing scenarios, based on the needs uncovered by research.

  - "Speed date" storyboards to a group of people followed by focus questions to help design teams understand what is in the users' minds.

  - Articulate misunderstandings, refine scenarios, and consider new design opportunities based on user rankings of needs and effectiveness.

  - Construct a simulated environment to allow people to act out a role from the revised scenarios, observing how users deal with specific problems in context.

See also   Experience Prototyping • Scenarios • Storyboards

ENACTMENT ONE:
THE PARENT BUTTON

What kinds of and how much virtual information can be comfortably displayed for parents to see?

ENACTMENT TWO:
MULTIPLE SELF-PRESENTATIONS

How would your different online personas look if they were all visible in one place?

Speed dating allows for structured engagements across multiple scenarios, creating new understanding about potential design opportunities to consider and problem areas that should be avoided.

101 Stakeholder Maps

A visual representation of key constituents of a design project

- Stakeholder maps provide a visual reference point for the design team, setting the stage for user-centered research and design development.

- Include people who will benefit from the project, those who hold power, those who may be adversely affected, and even those who may sabotage designed outcomes.

- Stakeholders can be identified by general roles (e.g., nurses), specific roles (e.g., chief of surgery), or by actual people (e.g., Linda, resident physician).

- From an initial sketch or list using whiteboards, cards, or paper, the map evolves into a structure with hierarchy and key relationships between roles or people.

- Stakeholder maps can take on a variety of forms, with a mix of text, photos, and graphics and use of scale, line, and proximity to express relationships.

See also   Stakeholder Walkthrough • Territory Maps

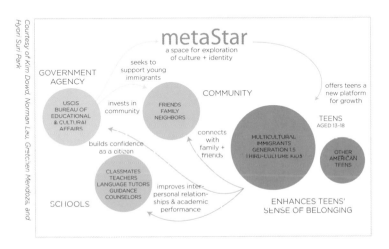

This is a stakeholder map consolidating key players and roles for the design of a social networking application for teenage immigrants during cultural transition to the United States.

102

Stakeholder Walkthrough

Early prototype evaluations by a team of end users, stakeholders, and designers

- The stakeholder walkthrough brings multiple stakeholders together to step through and evaluate a task-based scenario from the end user's perspective.

- As a group usability inspection method, it requires a diverse range of skills and perspectives to identify and consider problems early in the prototyping process.

- Attendees should be told that they will be asked to take the end user's perspective as opposed to defending a system or design/development view.

- The whole team works together, focusing on usability problem detection and brainstorming solutions.

- Team walkthroughs can be more costly than individual techniques, but they have proven to be more effective.

- Recurring attendance in stakeholder walkthroughs will sharpen the team's empathic response to their end user's frustrations, challenges, and perspectives.

See also   Design Charette • Stakeholder Maps • Usability Testing

projector screen

projector

interaction
designers

end users

developer

product managers

video recording device

Scheduling stakeholder walkthroughs early in the design
process combines perspectives of representative end users,
stakeholders, developers, and members of the design and
research team.

103

Storyboards

A visual narrative that generates empathy and communicates the context for proposed design solutions

- Five design practices common to visual storytelling:

  1. Refine drawings so that they show enough context, but not so much that details begin to distract from the purpose of the storyboard.

  2. Use text to supplement the visuals in a storyboard when it would otherwise take too much effort to illustrate a concept or idea.

  3. Emphasize people, products, or both, depending on whether you want to elicit an emotional impact or get technical or evaluative feedback on the concept.

  4. Use three to six panels to communicate an idea, with each storyboard focused on one salient concept.

  5. To show time lapses, use design elements such as clocks, calendars, or the movement of the sun.

See also   Personas • Role-playing • Speed Dating

Do you ever wish you had someone of a similar culture/background to talk with about type 2 diabetes?

Person is diagnosed with type 2 diabetes. Doctor leaves, and nurse comes in to set up the person with a mentor.

He or she inputs criteria for a mentor, and system finds a match with another person with type 2 diabetes.

The mentor answers questions as the person learns how to manage his or her diabetes.

Do you ever wish you had someone to help your spouse/family to understand what you are dealing with and how best to support you?

Family doesn't know how they can help their loved one with their type 2 diabetes.

Trained caregiver answers the family's questions and provides helpful tips to be supportive.

Family is active in providing care for their loved one.

Storyboards shape social, environmental, and temporal factors into a compelling narrative and help design teams to carefully consider how products and services could improve lives.

104

Surveys

Collection of self-reported information about thoughts, feelings, perceptions, behaviors, or attitudes

- A survey is an efficient tool for collecting a lot of versatile data in a short time frame, with results that can be analyzed statistically.

- Survey questionnaires can be either self-completed or read to participants and completed by the researcher.

- Interviews can be conducted in person, by phone, or through various communication technologies.

- Like any self-reporting, surveys may not accurately reflect true thoughts, feelings, perceptions, or behaviors.

- Surveys should therefore be carefully designed and administered and paired with complementary methods such as observations or contextual inquiry.

- There are various types of questions: closed/open, general/specific, factual, hypothetical, judgmental, and comparative.

- Questions should avoid leading to an answer or blaming the participant as wrong or at fault.

See also   Cultural Probes • Interviews • Questionnaires

The "Produce Proposal Wall" used a survey method allowing customers to communicate what they want in the grocery store, while fostering dialogue and building community.

105

Swimlanes

A holistic visualization of the activities of multiple actors in a flow of events

- Swimlanes can benefit any project where several processes or actors have to come together to shape the outcome of the same flow of events.

- Multiple swimlanes should be created from user research, each focused on its own specific story with the following elements:

  - **Storyboard lane:** Captures the events in a user story using comics, photographs, illustrations, or sketches.

  - **User Experience lane:** This is a flowchart depicting the story with more detail and insight into the process of the user experience.

  - **Business Process lane:** This is the business logic providing the required processes that facilitates the steps of the user experience.

  - **Tools and Systems lane:** Back-end technology that is involved to support user actions and business goals.

- The method visually connects an overarching user story with problems being solved at both a macro perspective and detailed micro view.

See also   Personas • Scenarios • Stakeholder Maps

The visual nature of swimlanes provides a bird's-eye view of the moving parts within a story, helping to get everyone on the same page.

106

Task Analysis

Workflow analysis, including user actions, system response, and environmental context

- *Task* encompasses any physical actions and mental processes as activities used to achieve goals and any information flows within the system environment.

- Designers typically incorporate a blend of qualitative and quantitative approaches to gain insight into user and task processes.

- The method targets user options, tools, decision points, common mistakes, corrections, inputs/outputs, frequency and importance of tasks, and risks of failure.

- Actions in task decomposition can be organized by categories, such as purpose, cues, objects, method, and options.

- A Hierarchical Task Analysis (HTA) typically results in tree diagrams or flowcharts, which can be verified by walk-through tests.

- Task analysis is useful for all design disciplines, ranging from navigation of software to wayfinding in the built environment.

See also   Contextual Inquiry • Ergonomic Analysis • Observation

A task analysis grid visualizes stakeholder scenarios and prioritized tasks. Each column describes a scenario, a task, and the subtasks necessary to complete the task.

107

Territory Maps

A visual representation of shared content focus to set research and design activities

- The creation process draws on the preconceptions and knowledge of design team members, contributed in a shared vision.

- The simplicity of the diagram is deceptively powerful, representing individual perspectives in a consensus artifact to foster design focus.

- The territory map serves a critical role in building team dynamic and cohesiveness for collaborative work.

- A speculative vision of the future is combined, including the key people who may be involved in the design landscape to be explored.

- Constructed early in the design process, during plan-ning, scoping, and definition, the map drives ideas for research and design.

- Territory maps may be drafted in a collaborative effort, or each member can consider their contributions first and then bring them to the group.

See also   Concept Mapping • Gap Analysis • Stakeholder Maps

Territory map for Grassroots, a project deploying sensors in the environment to help give neighbors a sense of community through shared data.

108

Thematic Networks

A step-by-step process to identify, organize, and connect common themes in qualitative data

- Systematically breaking down texts into patterns, themes, and relationships helps to synthesize qualitative information into actionable design insight.

- Three classes of themes summarize and organize information into a web-like illustration to communicate findings with stakeholders:

  1. Basic themes come directly from textual data, considered within the context of other basic themes to flesh out a fuller story.

  2. Organizing themes separate basic themes into clusters of similar issues, collectively forming a higher order premise as an argument, position, or assertion.

  3. Global themes distill the overarching point of the text into a single statement, articulating the deeper meaning and complexity of the data.

- Thematic networks help make sense of rich, textual data collected from methods such as diary studies, directed storytelling, or interviews.

See also Affinity Diagramming • Content Analysis • Exploratory Research

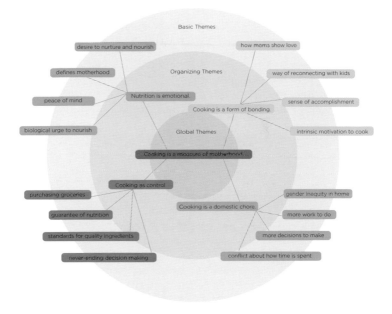

Basic Themes

Organizing Themes

Global Themes

- desire to nurture and nourish
- how moms show love
- defines motherhood
- way of reconnecting with kids
- peace of mind
- sense of accomplishment
- Nutrition is emotional.
- Cooking is a form of bonding.
- biological urge to nourish
- intrinsic motivation to cook

Cooking is a measure of motherhood.

- Cooking as control
- purchasing groceries
- gender inequity in home
- guarantee of nutrition
- Cooking is a domestic chore.
- more work to do
- standards for quality ingredients
- more decisions to make
- never-ending decision making
- conflict about how time is spent

Thematic network analysis provides a methodology that can help researchers work through the challenges of analyzing textual data using a formulaic, step-by-step methodology.

109

Think-aloud Protocol

A method where participants verbalize what they are doing and thinking as they complete a task

- Think-aloud Protocol is among the most common evaluative methods in the usability community, revealing aspects of an interface that delight, confuse, or frustrate.

- It asks people to articulate what they are doing, thinking, or feeling as they complete a set of tasks that align with their realistic day-to-day goals.

- Concurrent think-aloud is most common, asking the participant to work through tasks while articulating what he or she is doing, thinking, and feeling.

- Retrospective think-aloud asks participants to complete a task in silence and then comment on their processes as they watch a recorded replay of their experience. This can provide additional insight into participant reasoning, intentions, and strategy.

- The method can be used on low- or high-fidelity prototypes, physical artifacts that require assembly, devices to be synchronized, or customized products.

See also   Desirability Testing • Prototyping • Usability Testing

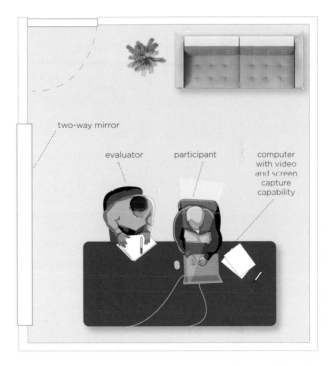

two-way mirror

evaluator   participant   computer
with video
and screen
capture
capability

In a think-aloud protocol, participants verbalize anything that
they think, feel, do, or look at while processing a prototype or
interface to complete tasks.

110

Time-aware Research

A moderated, remote testing method engaging a real person in real time, just as he or she is about to complete a task

- In contrast to traditional usability testing where tasks are preselected by researchers, time-aware research happens "just in time" to observe a task of interest.

- Live recruiting intercepts participants at the precise moment that they set out to complete a self-directed task, providing insight into how they accomplish goals.

- Using screen-sharing software, this method enables the usability test to occur within the context of an individual's native environment or "technological ecosystem."

- This is a more realistic process than lab testing, as participants can access information on websites, by email, or on their calendar.

- Around 1.5% to 2% of visitors who see the screener will complete it; slightly more than 50% will agree to be contacted; of those, around 65% will be able to participate.

See also   Experience Sampling Method • Remote Moderated Research • Usability Testing

In "live recruiting" for time-aware research, end users are intercepted by a prompt to participate in a study immediately as they begin a self-directed task.

111

Touchstone Tours

Using artifacts and the environment as touchstones for insightful conversation

- The guided tour is a contextual, empathic method to understand how people organize information and systems using space and cognitive artifacts.

- The exploratory method allows designers to establish familiarity with a territory in early-phase research.

- The participant is asked to guide the researcher through an environment and objects, specific to themes or subjects being explored by the designer.

- Tours can be guided through homes, workspaces or individual rooms, micro or mobile environments such as backpacks and purses, or digital devices and computer desktops.

- Conversation should be guided yet flexible, allowing fluid departures based on highlights selected by the tour guide and attentive observations by the researcher.

- Thoroughly document tours with video, photos, or sketches and a transcript of the conversation.

See also   Artifact Analysis • Contextual Inquiry • Personal Inventories

A touchstone tour in a prototyping lab highlights specialized tools and processes for a design project investigating master-apprentice relationships.

112

Transition Design

Design for systems-level change, addressing wicked problems to catalyze societal transitions toward more sustainable and desirable futures

- Transition design shares the objective of greater cultural and geographical diversity with initiatives to challenge the dominant U.S. and Eurocentric design paradigms.

- The designer acts as a facilitator, supporter, and bringer of resources and different forms of expertise to the community.

- Traditional design approaches are characterized by linear processes and de-contextualized problem frames, whose objective is usually the swift realization of predictable and profitable solutions.

- In contrast, transition design proposes that a more holistic approach is needed: systems change necessitates putting stakeholders at the heart of the problem-framing and problem-solving process, and systems interventions need to occur at multiple levels of scale and over short, medium, and long horizons of time.

Contributed by Gideon Kossoff and Terry Irwin

See also   Backcasting • Civic Design & Policy • Horizon Scanning

**Four mutually reinforcing and co-evolving areas
of knowledge, action, and self-reflection**

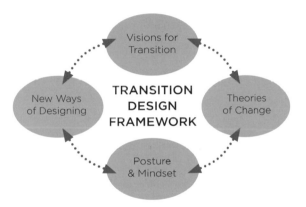

The Transition Design Framework brings together a body of
knowledge and skillsets in four key areas that are relevant to
design for systems-level change.

Courtesy of Terry Irwin

113

Tree Testing

A test of the organization and discoverability of content on a site by evaluating a text-based structure rather than a fully developed user interface

- Overlapping information categories and confusing labels remain two of the most pervasive problems in website design.

- Tree testing is usually done as a remote, unmoderated study using online software. To create a tree test, you need two things: the *tree* (the hierarchical, text-based representation of site navigation) and the *tasks* (the real-world situations that would motivate participants to look for certain information).

- The software presents the tree to the participants, and tracks how they move through the tree and which item they select as the destination for the task.

- Some basic metrics include the *breakdown of success* (how many people were successful in finding the information), *directness* (did people go directly to the destination), and *time taken* (how long did participants take to complete this task).

Contributed by Barbora Batokova

See also   Automated Remote Testing • Card Sorting • Content Inventory & Audit

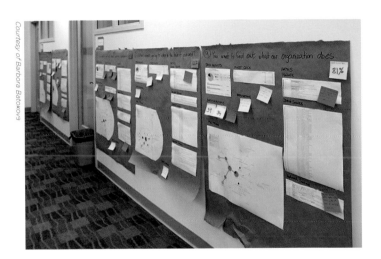

Creating a sheet of all types of results for each task allows for an easy analysis as well as sharing the results with others.

114

Triading

An interviewing technique whereby participants compare sets of three brands, products, or services

- Triading is a powerful interviewing technique that helps to understand how products and services fit into people's existing personal constructs of the world.

- Triading reveals deep-seated attitudes, perceptions, and feelings toward brands, products, and services.

- Either the researcher or the participant selects six to ten familiar and related brands, products, or services representative of a particular domain.

- The participant picks three of the examples (a triad) for discussion and then explains the ways in which they feel two of the three examples differ from the third.

- This process can be repeated with new triads to elicit multiple constructs about the domain.

- When repeated with many participants, a wealth of data emerges, with varied constructs and ratings identified from person to person.

See also   Interviews • Laddering • Semantic Differential

Triading asks: "How do two of these examples differ from the third?"

115

Triangulation

The convergence of multiple methods on the same research question to corroborate evidence from several different angles

- Triangulation ensures accuracy of information by combining sources and mitigating the weaknesses of any single method or source.

- The most common occurrence of triangulation is to combine behavioral observation methods with self-report methods such as questionnaires or interviews.

- Self-reported behaviors or attitudes aligned with social norms or research expectations may be contradicted by actual behaviors observed.

- Triangulation may compare physiological data such as heart rate or pupil dilation with self-reported information or observations of visible behaviors.

- Anecdotal information collected through qualitative means can enrich and humanize the abstraction of quantitative results collected through survey data.

- In usability studies, recordings are triangulated across keystroke/mouse inputs, facial expressions, and actions verbalized in think-aloud protocol.

See also Competitive Testing • Literature Reviews • Secondary Research

1. Observation data: Video capture   2. Behavioral data: Recorded TV interactions

3. Self-report data: Interviews

In a Microsoft study of television watching, observations and television interactions were used during interviews to correlate behaviors with TV content and events in the environment.

116

Unobtrusive Measures

Physical evidence, archival records, and nonintrusive observations used for design insight

- This method is used to acquire information without direct participant contact.

- Examples of physical trace *erosion* measures include wear patterns in floors or grass indicating preferred pedestrian traffic.

- Examples of *accretion* measures include litter, graffiti, temporary signage, product modifications, or fingerprints to indicate patterns of use.

- Archives are considered unobtrusive measures because they may be accessed without direct contact with participants.

- Observation can be an unobtrusive measure when those being observed do not know it and the researcher has had no input in the situation structure.

- Digital footprints provide indicators of technology use and qualities of social interaction and communication.

- A limitation may be a lack of details about who has contributed to the data being collected and why.

See also Artifact Analysis • Fly-on-the-Wall Observation • Secondary Research

Trace *erosion* measures are wear-patterns, such as these preferred pathways or "desire lines." Trace *accretion* measures include additive deposits such as graffiti and litter.

117

Usability Report

Empirical evidence outlining which parts of a user interface should be fixed or improved

- A usability report helps teams decide whether a product is usable enough to release or needs revision and further testing, through the following features:

  - Executive summary, describing the most salient and serious usability problems first, with sections tailored to the concerns of any specific groups

  - Total number of problems, including the frequency, impact, and persistence of usability problems, evidenced by screenshots, or participant quotes

  - A list of the most severe and persistent problems.

  - Positive findings that counterbalance problems with a similar number of observed interactions demonstrating good usability

  - Detailed task and scenario descriptions that are robust and representative enough to effectively get at a range of usability error types

See also   Remote Moderated Research • Think-aloud Protocol • Usability Testing

The proprietary platform of User Insight called "Voice" aggregates research documents, discussion guides, participant information, research calendars, and testing artifacts into a secure online repository.

118

Usability Testing

An evaluative method to observe a user's task-based experience with a digital applications

- Usability testing identifies frustrating and confusing parts of an interface so that they can be fixed and retested prior to launch.

- It typically employs Think-aloud Protocol, detecting problems by observing instances where the user:

  1. Understands the task but can't complete it within a reasonable amount of time

  2. Understands the goal, but has to try different approaches to complete the task

  3. Gives up or resigns from the process

  4. Completes a task, but not the specified task

  5. Expresses surprise or delight

  6. Expresses frustration, confusion, or blames themselves for not being able to complete the task

  7. Asserts that something is wrong or doesn't make sense

  8. Makes a suggestion for the interface or the flow of events

See also   Evaluative Research • Stakeholder Walkthrough • Think-aloud Protocol

Usability tests with few participants can isolate enough problems to help teams confidently decide whether an interface needs to be revised or is ready for release.

119

User Journey Maps

A visualization of human interactions with a
multi-channel product or service

- The journey map tells a visual story about an individual's
actions, feelings, perceptions, and mindset as they
interact with a product or service.

- It should be an honest representation of an experience,
including moments of indecision, confusion, frustration,
delight, and closure.

- The journey map allows each moment of an interactive
experience to be evaluated and improved by design.

- Multiple maps are usually created alongside personas
and scenarios, each heavily informed by direct contact
with customers who use the product or service.

- The journey map can shift an organization's focus from
an operational, system-centered view to the larger, real-
world context in which products and services are used.

- The map should be a living document, with reviews
by the design team offering questions, ideas, and
suggested improvements.

See also   Customer Experience Audit • Personas • Scenarios

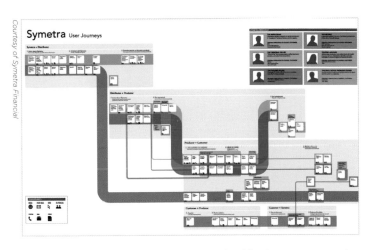

Interviews by digital agency POP resulted in six personas and journeys of Symetra Financial users, ultimately resulting in greater workflow efficiencies through a refreshed website design.

120

Value Opportunity Analysis (VOA)

Mapping the extent to which a product or service's aspirational qualities connect to an audience

- A VOA provides an opportunity for a team to work together from a place of deep empathy, grounded firmly in research for what the user values and desires.

- There are seven value opportunities:

  1. Emotion: *adventure, independence, confidence, and power*

  2. Aesthetics: *visual, auditory, tactile, olfactory, and taste*

  3. Identity: *point in time, sense of place, and personality*

  4. Impact: *social and environmental*

  5. Ergonomics: *comfort, safety, and ease of use*

  6. Core Technology: *reliable and enabling*

  7. Quality: *craftsmanship and durability*

- The VOA can be used to help the team consider competitive review, market analysis, and multiple personas.

See also Competitive Testing • Desirability Testing • The Love Letter & the Breakup Letter

In a VOA, each value opportunity and its attributes are listed in a column and rated on a subjective scale of low, medium, and high.

121

Values-based Assessment

An exploratory interview technique that structures discussion of "preference" by assessing concepts based on values that matter to participants

- There are five steps to conducting values-based assessments:

  1. Define no more than three to five values based on research about your participant segment's needs. These should include a mix of functional and emotional benefits or values. Print them on small cards.

  2. Ask participants to rank the values, describing out loud what each means to them in context, and focus the discussion on the higher-ranked values.

  3. To set up the assessment space, use a long piece of blue painter's tape on a table where the participant will sit. At opposite ends, place the cards.

  4. Ask participants to place concepts freely along a spectrum created by the blue line.

  5. Wrap up by revisiting the concepts without the values to understand what influences a participant.

Contributed by Pete Weeks

See also   Card Sorting • Picture Cards • Triading

1. Design concepts are initially hidden, allowing focus on values.

2. Participant sorts Values Cards representing functional and emotional beliefs.

3. Design concepts are revealed in tangible form, and then evaluated.

4. The moderator observes and discusses assessments.

122

Web Analytics

The collection and analysis of Internet data to understand and optimize web usage

- This process provides a gateway for your organization to become invested in what your customers are doing online and why.

- The first step requires articulating what you want out of the data, expressing your goals and intent for what you want to measure.

- Knowing where you want to go can help you structure your content, analyze campaigns, segment your visitors, and measure your commerce and process tools.

- Translate all of the data into a short report people will want to read, avoiding analytics jargon and visualizing as much data as you can.

- Regularly share reports to internal stakeholders.

- Implement and act on the knowledge, focusing on small course corrections that can have a big impact.

See also   A/B Testing • Key Performance Indicators • Site Search Analytics

Web analysts will understand your business and the web in equal measure and use tools such as Google Analytics to make recommendations for corrective actions.

123

Weighted Matrix

Identify and prioritize the most promising opportunities from multiple design concepts

- A weighted matrix creates a forum for conversation and shared decision- making and can help overcome the common biases on multidisciplinary teams.

- The underlying concept is simple but powerful: the matrix ranks potential design opportunities against key success criteria.

- The "criteria" represents the primary measures of product success rated on a scale, as defined by the product team and organizational stakeholders.

- A listing of "opportunities" represents the design ideas that elicit the most serious interest from the team.

- Once there is an agreed-upon recommended list, another creative "deep dive" can now refocus on newly agreed-upon design ideas.

- The method provides a structured process for team conversations, shifting decision-making to a process grounded in success criteria, not personal opinions.

See also Design Charette • KJ Technique • Parallel Prototyping

IDEAS → BUSINESS CRITERA ↓	WEIGHT	Cargo Organizers	Non-car Accessories	Travel Accessories	Mobilizing Medical Devices	Child Transport
Within Our Companies' Expertise	3	2	3	3	2	2
User Experience	3	2	2	1	3	3
Potential Market Size	2	2	2	3	1	2
Potential for Market Differentiation	2	1	1	2	2	3
Industry Recognition	1	1	1	2	3	3
TOTALS		19	22	24	24	(28)

BUSINESS CRITERA	WEIGHT	Work Benches	Garage Storage	Rugged Mobility Devices
Within Our Companies' Expertise	3	3	3	2
User Experience	3	2	3	2
Potential Market Size	2	1	3	1
Potential for Market Differentiation	2	1	2	2
Industry Recognition	1	1	2	3
TOTALS		20	(30)	21

A weighted matrix provides a way to manage potential design options by evaluating each design opportunity against business criteria as opposed to personal preferences.

124

Wizard of Oz

Simulated control and response by a researcher behind the scenes, while a participant engages with a system

- Participants are led to believe they are interacting with a working prototype, but in reality, a researcher is acting as a proxy from behind the scenes.

- The "wizard" can intercept and shape the interaction between the participant and the system.

- The goal is to allow a user to realistically experience a product or interface before prototypes are built.

- For an appropriate, timely system response, the researcher must observe participant activity: for example, through video or screen-sharing software.

- The believability of the simulations hinge on the wizard's consistency with respect to timing, patterns, and system logic.

- This is useful when designing applications that do not already have established design patterns (for example, augmented reality or ubiquitous computing).

See also   Experience Prototyping •
Rapid Iterative Testing & Evaluation • Speed Dating

Thousands of people have had compelling interactions with the animatronic character Quasi the Robot without knowing that behind the scenes, a human actor controls the robot.

125

Word Clouds

Information visualization that organizes text-based content into interesting arrangements

- Word clouds are text collages that show the most frequently used words in just about any text-based document.

- Words are assigned different font sizes; usually, the bigger the word, the more frequently it occurs.

- Clouds are made engaging through various dimensions such as typeface, font size, colors, and number of words, word proximity, and word orientation.

- Qualify where word cloud data came from, collection methods, what the fonts, colors, sizes, etc. mean, and disclosure of any data scrubbing or segmenting.

- When archiving transcripts, the visual markers of each cloud create a gestalt unique to each transcript that can facilitate recall.

- Word clouds can be a lighthearted way to engage stakeholders in discussion about the gist of transcripts before delving into more rigorous analysis techniques.

See also   Content Analysis • Exploratory Research • Interviews

Here is a word cloud generated from interviews with parents of picky eaters. When segmented based on meaningful criteria, word clouds can reveal potentially insightful and surprising themes.

References & Notes

05 Automated Remote Research
Bolt, N., and T. Tulathimutte. *Remote Research: Real Users, Real Time, Real Research*. Brooklyn, NY: Rosenfeld Media, 2010.

07 Behavioral Design
Tromp, N., and P. Hekkert. *Designing for Society: Products and Services for a Better World*. London: Bloomsbury, 2018.

08 Behavioral Mapping
Sommer, R., and B. Sommer. *A Practical Guide to Behavioral Research: Tools and Techniques*. New York, NY: Oxford University Press, 2002.

09 Blockbusting
Adams, J. L. *Conceptual Blockbusting: A Guide to Better Ideas*. WW Norton & Company, 1980.

10 Bodystorming
Burns, C., et al. "Actors, Hairdos & Videotape—Informance Design: Using Performance Techniques in Multidisciplinary, Observation-based Design." In *CHI 94 Conference Companion*, 1994: 119–120.

11 Brainstorm Graphic Organizers
Hyerle, D. *Visual Tools for Constructing Knowledge*. Alexandria, VA: ASCD, 1996.

12 Brand Experience Workshop
The Brand Experience Workshop method was developed by and is taught by Cooper, www.cooper.com.

Design Leadership Cards, Cooper. (Obtained from the Design Leadership workshop by Cooper.)

13 Bull's-Eye Diagramming
Bull's-Eye Diagramming is a method from the LUMA System of Innovation. To learn more, visit www.luma-institute.com/why-luma/our-system/.

"Bull's-Eye Diagramming." LUMA Institute. *Innovating for People: Handbook of Human-Centered Design*. LUMA Institute, 2012.

"What's on Your Radar?" LUMA Institute. *Innovating for People: Handbook of Human-Centered Design*. LUMA Institute, 2012.

16 Case Studies
Robson, C. *Real World Research: A Resource for Social Scientists and Practitioner-Researchers*, 2nd ed. Oxford: Blackwell Publishers, 2002.

18 Cognitive Mapping
Ackermann, F., et al. "Getting Started with Cognitive Mapping" in *The Young OR Conference, University of Warwick*, 1992: 65–82.

19 Cognitive Walkthrough
Wharton, C., et al. "The Cognitive Walkthrough: A Practitioner's Guide" in *Usability Inspection Methods*. New York, NY: John Wiley and Sons, 1994.

25 Contextual Design
Holtzblatt, K., et al. *Rapid Contextual Design: A How-To Guide to Key Techniques for User-Centered Design*. San Francisco, CA: Morgan Kaufmann, 2004.

26 Contextual Inquiry
Holtzblatt, K., and H. Beyer. *Contextual Design: A Customer-Centered Approach to Systems Design*. San Francisco, CA: Morgan Kaufmann, 1998.

27 Creative Matrix
Creative Matrix is a method from the LUMA System of Innovation. To learn more, visit www.luma-institute.com/why luma/our-system/.

LUMA Institute. *Innovating for People: Handbook of Human-Centered Design*. LUMA Institute, 2012.

30 Critiques
Lerman, L., and J. Borstel. *Liz Lerman's Critical Response Process: A Method for Getting Useful Feedback on Anything You Make, from Dance to Dessert*. Takoma Park, MD: Dance Exchange, 2003.

31 Crowdsourcing
Kittur, A. et al. "Crowdsourcing for Usability: Using Micro-Task Markets for Rapid, Remote, and Low-Cost User Measurements," 2008, www.researchgate.net/publication/228917129

32 Cultural Probes
Gaver, B., et al. "Cultural Probes." *Interactions*, January-February 1999, pp. 21–29.

34 Data Physicalization
Nissen, B., and J. Bowers. "Data-Things: Digital Fabrication Situated Within Participatory Data Translation Activities." In *Proceedings of the 33rd Annual ACM Conference on Human Factors in Computing Systems (CHI 2015)*. New York: ACM, 2015: 2467–2476.

35 Data Visualization
Norman, D. *Things That Make Us Smart: Defending Human Attributes in the Age of the Machine*. Diversion Books, 2014.

Wurman, R. S., et al. *Information Anxiety 2*. Que, 2001.

Yau, N. *Data Points: Visualization That Means Something*. John Wiley & Sons, 2013.

38 Design Fiction
Dunne, A., and F. Raby. *Speculative Everything*. Cambridge, MA: MIT Press, 2013.

Sterling, B. *Design Fiction: Anticonventional Objects*. (2013, October 10) Wired.com. www.wired.com/2013/10/design-fiction-anticonventional-objects/

40 Desirability Testing
Barnum, C. M., and L. A. Palmer. "More Than a Feeling: Understanding the Desirability Factor in User Experience." in *Proceedings of CHI 2010* (2010): 4703–4715.

42 Directed Storytelling
Evenson, S. "Directed Storytelling: Interpreting Experience for Design" in *Design Studies: Theory and Research in Graphic Design, A Reader.* New York, NY: Princeton Architectural Press, 2006: 231–240.

43 Drawing
Baskinger, M., and W. Bardel. *Drawing Ideas: A Hand-drawn Approach for Better Design.* Watson-Guptill, 2013.

44 Elito Method
Ulrich, E. "Inclusive Iterations: How a Design Team Builds Shared Insights." *UX Week Podcast,* 2007.

45 Empathy Maps
The empathy map was originally created by Dave Gray and collaborators at XPLANE, situated in a larger set of human-centered research and design tools called "Gamestorming." See: gamestorming.com

In an interesting example of human-centered design thinking, Dave Gray iterated on the empathy map based on versions proliferating on the internet, with input from users of the canvas.

See: https://medium.com/the-xplane-collection/updated-empathy-map-canvas-46df22df3c8a

46 Ergonomic Analysis
Tannen, R. "Crimping Tools: An Ergonomic Review of the State-of-the-Art." White paper for Thomas & Betts, June 2009.

48 Evidence-based Design
Scupelli, P., et al. "Architecture and Information Technology as Factors in Surgical Suite Information Sharing and Coordination." in *Proceedings of the 1st ACM International Health Informatics Symposium,* 2010: 265–274.

49 Experience Prototyping
Buchenau, M., and J. F. Suri. "Experience Prototyping" in *Proceedings of Designing Interactive Systems (DIS).* ACM, 2000: 424–433.

51 Experiments
Larson, A. M., and L. C. Loschky. "The Contributions of Central Versus Peripheral Vision to Scene Gist Recognition." *Journal of Vision* 9, no. 10 (2009): 1–16.

55 Fly-on-the-Wall Observation
Zeisel, J. *Inquiry by Design: Environment/ Behavior/Neuroscience in Architecture, Interiors, Landscape, and Planning.* New York, NY: Norton, 2006.

57 Gap Analysis
Anderson, L. W., et al. *A Taxonomy for Learning, Teaching, and Assessing:*

A Revision of Bloom's Taxonomy of Educational Objectives. Abridged edition. White Plains, NY: Longman, 2001.

Dirksen, J. *Design for How People Learn.* New Riders, 2015.

Gery, G. J. *Electronic Performance Support Systems: How and Why to Remake the Workplace through the Strategic Application of Technology.* Weingarten Publications, Inc., 1991.

60 Heuristic Evaluation
Ginsburg, S. *Designing the iPhone User Experience.* Boston, MA: Addison Wesley, 2010.

Nielsen, J. *Usability Engineering.* Boston, MA: Academic Press, 1993.

62 Horizon Scanning
Molitor, G. "How to Anticipate Public Policy Changes." *S.A.M Advanced Management Journal* 42, no. 3 (1977): 4–13.

Schultz, W. "The Cultural Contradictions of Managing Change: Using Horizon Scanning in an Evidence-Based Policy Context." *Foresight* 8, no. 4 (2006): 3–12.

See: https://thinkingfutures.net/

63 How Might We
How Might We or HMW is credited to the business consultant Min Basadur, who in the early 1970s introduced it while working as a creative manager at Proctor and Gamble. The method spread through its proponents to Scient, IDEO, Google, Facebook, and gradually even to the nonprofit sector. For a concise history, see https://toolkit.mozilla.org/method/how-might-we/

65 Importance-Difficulty Matrix
Utilizing a two-axis chart to assess the return on investment or cost-benefit of addressing various usability issues was proposed and documented by MAYA Design, laying the foundation for widespread use of the Importance-Difficulty Matrix. See: McQuaid, H., and D. Bishop. "An Integrated Method for Evaluating Interfaces." *Usability Professionals' Association Conference Proceedings*, 2001.

67 KJ Technique
Kawakita, J. *The Original KJ Method.* Tokyo: Kawakita Research Institute, 1982.

Spool, J. "The KJ-Technique: A Group Process for Establishing Priorities," 2004, www.uie.com

68 Kano Analysis
Kano, N., et al. "Attractive Quality and Must-be Quality." *Journal of the Japanese Society for Quality Control* 14, no. 2 (1984): 39–48.

Zultner, R. E., and G. H. Mazur. "The Kano Model: Recent Developments." in *The Eighteenth Symposium on Quality Function Deployment*, 2006: 109–116.

69 Key Performance Indicators
Peterson, E. *The Big Book of Key Performance Indicators*, 2006, www.webanalyticsdemystified.com/downloads/The_Big_Book_of_Key_Performance_Indicators_by_Eric_Peterson.pdf

70 Laddering
Reynolds, T. J., and J. Gutman. "Laddering Theory, Method, Analysis, and Interpretation." *Journal of Advertising Research* 28 (1988): 11–31.

Wansink, B., and N. Chan. "Using Laddering to Understand and Leverage a Brand's Equity." *Qualitative Market Research—An International Journal* 6, no.2 (2003).

72 The Love Letter & the Breakup Letter
https://vimeo.com/11854531

73 Mental Model Diagrams
Young, I. *Mental Models: Aligning Design Strategy with Human Behavior*. Brooklyn, NY: Rosenfeld Media, 2008.

74 Metaphors
Burke, K. *A Grammar of Motives*. New Jersey: Prentice-Hall, 1945.

Cila, N. *Metaphors We Design By: The Use of Metaphors in Product Design*. Ph.D. thesis, TU Delft, 2013.

75 Mind Mapping
Hyerle, D. *Visual Tools for Constructing Knowledge*. Alexandria, VA: ASCD, 1996.

77 Parallel Prototyping
Dow, S. P., et al. "Parallel Prototyping Leads to Better Design Results, More Divergence, and Increased Self-Efficacy." *ACM Transactions on Computer-Human Interaction* 17, no. 4 (2010).

78 Participant Observation
Zeisel, J. *Inquiry by Design: Environment/Behavior/Neuroscience in Architecture, Interiors, Landscape, and Planning*. New York: Norton, 2006.

79 Participatory Action Research (PAR)
McNiff, J. *Action Research for Professional Development*, 2002, www.jeanmcniff.com/ar-booklet.asp

80 Participatory Design
Kuhn, S., and T. Winograd. "Participatory Design" in *Bringing Design to Software*, New York: Addison-Wesley, 1996.

Sanders, E. B.-N., et al. "A Framework for Organizing the Tools and Techniques of Participatory Design" in *Participatory Design Conference (PDC) Proceedings*, 2010: 195–198.

81 Personal Inventories
Blevis, E., and E. Stolterman. "Ensoulment and Sustainable Interaction Design" in *Proceedings of International Association of Design Research Societies Conference IASDR 2007*. Hong Kong(China): HKPT, 2007.

82 Personas
Cooper, A. *The Inmates Are Running the Asylum: Why High-Tech Products Drive Us Crazy and How to Restore the Sanity.* Indianapolis, IN: Sams–Pearson Education, 2004.

84 Picture Cards
The Picture Cards method was developed by Adaptive Path, www.adaptivepath.com

Kaptelinin, V., and B. A. Nardi. *Acting with Technology: Activity Theory and Interaction Design.* Cambridge, MA: The MIT Press, 2006.

87 Rapid Iterative Testing & Evaluation
Schrag, J. "Using Formative Usability Testing as a Fast UI Design Tool." *UPA Conference Proceedings*, 2006.

88 Remote Moderated Research
Bolt, N., and T. Tulathimutte. *Remote Research: Real Users, Real Time, Real Research.* San Francisco, CA: Rosenfeld Media, 2010.

89 Research Through Design
Burdick, A. "Design (as) Research" in *Design Research: Methods and Perspectives*, Cambridge, MA: MIT Press, 2003: 82.

Zimmerman, J., et al. "Research Through Design as a Method for Interaction Design Research in HCI." In *Proceedings of CHI*, ACM, 2007: 493-502.

91 Rose Thorn Bud
The Rose Thorn Bud method is borrowed from the Boy Scouts of America, who use the method to encourage scouts to identify within situations they encounter a positive experience (Rose), a negative experience (Thorn), and a new goal or insight (Bud). Pete Lucas of MAYA Design, himself a scout leader, crossed the technique over as a design method. See *Innovating for People: Handbook of Human-Centered Design.* LUMA Institute, 2012.

94 Semantic Differential
Osgood, C., et al. *The Measurement of Meaning.* Urbana, IL: University of Illinois Press, 1957.

95 Service Blueprint
Kimbell, L. *The Service Innovation Handbook: Action-Oriented Creative Thinking Toolkit for Service Organizations.* Amsterdam: BIS, 2016.

96 Service Design
Guilford, J. P. "The Structure of Intellect." *Psychological Bulletin* 53, no. 4 (1956): 267.

Kimbell, L. *The Service Innovation Handbook: Action-Oriented Creative Thinking Toolkit for Service Organizations.* Amsterdam: BIS, 2016.

Meroni, A., and D. Sangiorgi, eds. *Design for Services.* Gower Publishing, 2012.

99 Site Search Analytics
Rosenfeld, L. *Search Analytics for Your Site: Conversations With Your Customers.* Brooklyn, NY: Rosenfeld Media, 2011.

100 Speed Dating
Davidoff, S., et al. "Rapidly Exploring Application Design Through Speed Dating." in *Proceedings of 9th International Conference on Ubiquitous Computing UbiComp '07,* 2007: 429–446.

102 Stakeholder Walkthrough
Karat, C.-M., et al. "Comparison of Empirical Testing and Walkthrough Methods in User Interface Evaluation." in *Proceedings of the SIGCHI Conference on Human Factors in Computing Systems,* 1992: 397–404.

103 Storyboards
Truong, K. N., et al. "Storyboarding: An Empirical Determination of Best Practices and Effective Guidelines." in *Proceedings of DIS 2006,* 2006: 12–21.

105 Swimlanes
Yvonne Shek at nForm adapted swimlanes as an activity diagram of the Unified Modeling Language (UML) in 2007.

106 Task Analysis
Kirwan, B., and L. K. Ainsworth. *A Guide to Task Analysis.* London; Washington D.C.: Taylor and Francis, 1992: 397–404.

Kuniavsky, M. *Observing the User Experience: A Practitioner's Guide to User Research.* San Francisco, CA: Morgan Kaufmann, 2003.

108 Thematic Networks
Attride-Stirling, J. "Thematic Networks: An Analytic Tool for Qualitative Research." *Qualitative Research* 1, no. 3 (2001): 385–405.

109 Think-aloud Protocol
Guan, Z., et al. "The Validity of Stimulated Retrospective Think-Aloud Method as Measured by Eye Tracking." in *CHI 2006 Conference Proceedings,* 2006: 1253–1262.

110 Time-aware Research
Bolt, N., and T. Tulathimutte. *Remote Research: Real Users, Real Time, Real Research.* Brooklyn, NY: Rosenfeld Media, 2010.

113 Tree Testing
See: https://www.nngroup.com/articles/top-10-enduring/

116 Unobtrusive Measures
Webb, E. J., et al. *Unobtrusive Measures: Nonreactive Research in the Social Sciences.* Chicago: Rand McNally, 1966. Revised edition, Thousand Oaks, CA: Sage Publications, 2000.

118 Usability Testing
Jacobson, N. E., et al. "The Evaluator Effect in Usability Studies: Problem Detection and Severity Judgments." in *Proceedings of the Human Factors and Ergonomics Society 42nd Annual Meeting*, 1998: 1336–1340.

120 Value Opportunity Analysis
Cagan, J., and C. Vogel. *Creating Breakthrough Products: Innovation from Product Planning to Program Approval.* Upper Saddle River, NJ: Prentice Hall, 2002.

121 Values-based Assessment
Values-based assessments were developed by a number of practitioners who needed to understand how new-to-world concepts met participant needs, when some of those needs were not obvious to the participants themselves. Design thinkers at Boston-area consultancy Continuum call this method Resonance Testing, as they seek to test which concepts resonate with different customer values.

122 Web Analytics
Peterson, E. *Web Analytics Demystified*, 2004, www.webanalyticsdemystified.com

Burby, J. *Three Reasons Analytics Fail Companies*, 2004, www.clickz.com

123 Weighted Matrix
Cagan, J., and C. Vogel. *Creating Breakthrough Products: Innovation from Product Planning to Program Approval.* Upper Saddle River, NJ: Prentice Hall, 2002.

124 Wizard of Oz
Kelly, J. F. "An Iterative Design Methodology for User-Friendly Natural Language Office Information Applications." *ACM Transactions on Office Information Systems* 2, no. 1 (1984): 26–41.

Inspiring | Educating | Creating | Entertaining

Brimming with creative inspiration, how-to projects, and useful information to enrich your everyday life, Quarto Knows is a favorite destination for those pursuing their interests and passions. Visit our site and dig deeper with our books into your area of interest: Quarto Creates, Quarto Cooks, Quarto Homes, Quarto Lives, Quarto Drives, Quarto Explores, Quarto Gifts, or Quarto Kids.

10 9 8 7 6 5 4 3 2 1

ISBN: 978-0-7603-7214-2

Cover: Coa Design

Page Layout: *tabula rasa* graphic design

Printed in China

This book is dedicated to Lauren Chapman Ruiz
Designer | Researcher | Teacher | Friend